The Life and Ministry of
JESUS CHRIST

Leader's Resource

BRINGING TRUTH TO LIFE
NavPress Publishing Group
P.O. Box 35001, Colorado Springs, Colorado 80935

The Navigators is an international Christian organization. Our mission is to reach, disciple, and equip people to know Christ and to make Him known through successive generations. We envision multitudes of diverse people in the United States and every other nation who have a passionate love for Christ, live a lifestyle of sharing Christ's love, and multiply spiritual laborers among those without Christ.

NavPress is the publishing ministry of The Navigators. NavPress publications help believers learn biblical truth and apply what they learn to their lives and ministries. Our mission is to stimulate spiritual formation among our readers.

ISBN 08910-99662

Map: GeoSystems Global Corporation

This series was produced for NavPress with the assistance of The Livingstone Corporation. James C. Galvin, Valerie Weidemann, and Daryl J. Lucas, project editors.

Printed in the United States of America

1 2 3 4 5 6 7 8 9 10 11 12 13 14 15 / 99 98 97 96

CONTENTS

CHALLENGING TRADITION

THE MESSIAH

FOLLOWING JESUS

ANSWERING THE CALL

FINAL TEACHINGS

INTRODUCTION

If your small group members want to learn more about Jesus Christ and become more like Him, then THE LIFE AND MINISTRY OF JESUS CHRIST series is for you. The seven-book Bible study spans all four Gospels, covers the entire life of Christ in chronological order, and emphasizes personal application of biblical truth. By using an inductive study format, THE LIFE AND MINISTRY OF JESUS CHRIST helps each person investigate what Jesus did and what He taught.

Each guide has five lessons and may be studied in five sessions, or in as many as ten to twelve sessions if your group prefers a slower pace. For best results, each group member should study the passages listed and write out the answers to the questions—including the application questions in the side columns. Then, in your group meeting, discuss together what each of you has observed and applied. The side columns can also be used to write additional insights or applications that emerge from the discussion. The emphasis on application helps to maintain a balance between factual knowledge and character development. Investing more time and prayer in the study leads to gaining greater benefits from it.

In each section of a given lesson, one biblical passage will be the main focus of study. That passage is printed in the guides and featured on the contents pages of this resource. Additional passages may also be listed. Group members should read them as they have time.

The Scripture passages were arranged based on the order presented by A. T. Robertson in *A Harmony of the Gospels* (Harper & Brothers, 1950). A harmony is a sequencing of the four Gospel accounts of the life of Jesus in parallel form to facilitate a study of His life and ministry. The harmony used in this study, "Harmony of the Life and Ministry of Jesus Christ," is in the back of each study guide.

A harmony shows the events in the life of Christ in chronological order. Some events, such as the feeding of the five thousand, are recorded in all four Gospels; others, such as Jesus' interview with Nicodemus in the Gospel of John, appear in only one. Mark's Gospel is the most chronological; Matthew's follows themes more closely than chronology.

Without careful study and the aid of a harmony, the Gospels may appear to contain chronological discrepancies. The order of the material in each Gospel differs because Jesus taught the same truths, told the same parables, and performed similar miracles many times in His three-and-a-half year ministry. So Matthew recorded the contents of the Sermon on the Mount in one large section toward the beginning of Jesus' ministry (Matthew 5–7), while Luke wrote down similar teachings of Jesus throughout His ministry (Luke 6:17-49, 11:1-13, 13:22-30). Undoubtedly Jesus pronounced judgment on those who opposed and harassed Him a number of times, so Matthew tells of an incident in Galilee toward the middle of His ministry (Matthew 12:22-45) while Luke records another such confrontation, this time in Judea, later in His ministry (Luke 11:14-36). These are not contradictions but records of similar events.

This Bible study resulted from the diligent work of many men and women around the world. A team of Navigator staff realized the need for this study and began putting it together. Others field tested the material and made refinements. Still others read it and offered valuable advice. Then skilled editors shaped the study to its final form.

To all who have prayed and labored diligently, a hearty word of thanks. It is, in every sense, the result of a team effort, coached and coordinated by the Holy Spirit. As the Author of the Word of God, as Teacher and Interpreter of the Word to believers, and as the Divine Distributor of His gifts to them, the Holy Spirit has in a unique way directed the production of this study. His desire for its effectiveness must stem from His special ministry of revealing and glorifying Jesus Christ in our lives. To this purpose the study is dedicated.

> *"I have much more to say to you, more than you can now bear. But when he, the Spirit of truth, comes, he will guide you into all truth. He will not speak on his own; he will speak only what he hears, and he will tell you what is yet to come. He will bring glory to me by taking from what is mine and making it known to you. All that belongs to the Father is mine. That is why I said the Spirit will take from what is mine and make it known to you." (John 16:12-15)*

The Beginning

THE BEGINNING

LESSON ONE

THE TRUTH ABOUT JESUS

As you begin this study, keep in mind that each participant comes with a different perspective of who Jesus is. Some will know a lot about Christ, others very little. Some may have misconceptions that need to be corrected. In this first lesson, you'll begin to discover what each person hopes to learn from this series. Listen carefully as the individuals in your group reveal their expectations and needs—this will help you prepare for future lessons.

OBJECTIVE: As a result of this lesson, participants will be introduced to the authors of the four Gospels and will understand how Jesus' message is relevant to us.

Opening Questions

- If a famous person asked you to write his biography, how would you go about doing it?
- How would you feel if someone wanted to publish your life story?

THE MEN WHO WROTE THE GOSPELS

Mark 1:1, Luke 1:1-4

Additional Information

As you compare the four Gospel accounts of Christ's life, you will find that each offers a different perspective. The first three Gospels are somewhat similar and are called the Synoptics, because of their essential parallel content. The Gospel of John is different in many ways, containing incidents not found in the other three.

When more than one writer chose to include the same event, the accounts often differ in perspective and content. This is not because the writers disagreed on the facts, but because each author had a different relationship to Jesus and a different purpose for writing.

Because the writers presented Jesus as the Christ to a different group of people, each Gospel contains a different emphasis. The Gospel of Matthew was addressed primarily to Jews, and emphasized Jesus as the King. The approach of the writer was to show Jesus fulfilling Old Testament prophecies, to present His teachings topically, and to contrast Him with the Pharisees.

The Gospel of Mark was addressed mainly to the Romans, and emphasized Jesus as the Servant. Mark recorded the actions of Jesus more than His teachings, explained Jewish traditions, and concentrated on His power and authority.

The Gospel of Luke was written to the Greeks or Gentiles of a Greek mind-set, and emphasized Jesus as a true Man. It is scholarly and historical, deals with human needs, and presents the human side of the Son of God.

The Gospel of John was addressed to the world, and emphasized Jesus as God. The writer builds belief in Jesus as the incarnate Son of God, shows Jesus as being independent from human influence, and presents Jesus' teachings more than His actions.

Additional Questions

- ▶What natural talents, character traits, and experience do you think qualified these four men to write the Gospels?
- ▶Do you think God usually looks for natural abilities when He chooses a person to do a job for Him? Why, or why not?
- ▶How can four different versions of the same events all be accurate?
- ▶How do you think the Gospel writers personally benefited from recording the events in Jesus' life?
- ▶In what ways do you think a spiritual journal would help you?
- ▶To what extent do you think we should tailor the gospel message to meet the different needs of people?

GOD BECAME A HUMAN BEING
John 1:1-18

Additional Information

The prologue to John's Gospel clearly presents the essential deity of the Messiah. In profound theological language, John shows Jesus' divinity and preexistence. Philippians 2:6-7 and Colossians 1:15-20 further explain the Incarnation (the Son of God taking on a human body and human nature). Though difficult to grasp, this truth is essential to the Christian faith. As you lead your group through this passage, keep in mind that we don't have to fully understand the mystery of the Incarnation to believe that it is true.

Additional Questions

- What did Christ give up to become a man?
- How can we reconcile Christ's kingship with His suffering and death?
- How is the truth of the Incarnation essential to our faith?
- What can we do when we don't understand difficult theological concepts?

THE ANCESTORS OF JESUS
Matthew 1:1-17, Luke 3:23-38

Additional Information

God gave His promises to specific people, so that when Jesus came He could be clearly identified as the Messiah. The divinely planned genealogies in the Gospels of Matthew and Luke substantiate Jesus' claims that He was the long-awaited promised Messiah.

Matthew traces the legal, or royal, ancestry of the Messiah through Joseph, Jesus' legal father, beginning with Abraham; his Gospel was primarily written to the Jews. Beginning with Adam, Luke traces the physical, or priestly, line of Jesus through Mary, His physical mother; his Gospel was mainly written to the Gentiles.

The two genealogies are identical from Abraham to David, where they diverge to follow the lines of two sons of the great king of Israel. They merge again during the Babylonian captivity.

Often generations were purposely left out, as Matthew did when he arranged his genealogy in groups of fourteen names. ("Son of" can mean either son or descendant.) Some scholars believe these divisions made for easier memorization by the early Church;

others feel the genealogy was divided according to the three periods of Jewish national history. Genealogies in Israel were public records, and Jews have never questioned the lineage of Jesus. Many Bible readers skip over these accounts and thus miss some of the interesting people mentioned in the messianic line. A careful study of Matthew's genealogy, for example, shows how God breaks down the barriers between Jew and Gentile, between male and female, and between saint and sinner.

Additional Questions

- Which names do you recognize in these family histories?
- What characteristics do these people have in common?
- How do you see God's grace and sovereignty at work in the ancestry of Jesus?
- What do these genealogies reveal about the kind of people God chooses to work through?
- In what ways do we hinder God's work in our lives?
- In your opinion, what is the most convincing evidence that Jesus is the Son of God?

NEXT TIME: One might think that God would choose the world's most important and powerful people to welcome His only Son into the world. But God had a better plan. As you prepare for your next meeting, you'll be surprised and encouraged to discover the kinds of people God used to carry out His plan of salvation.

THE BEGINNING

LESSON TWO

BREAKING THE SILENCE

During what has been called the inter-testamental period, the nation of Israel had not heard from the Lord either through angels or prophets. This 400-year silence was broken when an angel promised the birth of the Messiah's forerunner to Zechariah. As you study the announcements of the angels and the births of both John the Baptist and Jesus, watch for similarities in the way in which God chose to reveal His plan to the world.

OBJECTIVE: As a result of this lesson, participants will see how God used ordinary, but faithful, people to bring about His plan of salvation for the world.

Opening Questions

- What different emotions often follow the announcement, "You're going to have a baby!"?
- How do families usually prepare for the birth of a child?

AN ANGEL PROMISES THE BIRTH OF JOHN TO ZECHARIAH

Luke 1:5-25

Additional Information

"Zacharias [Zechariah] was a member of the course of Abijah, one of the twenty-four clans or ranks of priests who maintained the Temple ritual (I Chron. 24:10). The 'courses' took turns in conducting the ceremonies of worship and each member usually had the privilege of presiding once in his lifetime (I Chronicles 24:19). The opportunity of offering incense was the high point of Zacharias' career, for he was delegated to enter into the holy place of the Temple, where the altar of incense stood before the mysterious veil that concealed the Holy of Holies."[1]

"For the Jews, children had always been considered as a blessing and as the highest form of wealth. One psalm said 'Fatherhood itself is the Lord's gift, the fruitful womb is a reward that comes from Him,' and another compared the father of a large family to a man whose table is surrounded by young olives (Psalms 126 and 127). . . . Barrenness, then, was a standing shame, as Elizabeth, John the Baptist's mother, said in so many words (Luke 1:25); and the rabbis went farther, stating that 'a childless man should be thought of as dead.' As for voluntary sterility, it was so grave a sin that the prophet Isaiah came to call the king Hezekiah to account for it, telling him that death was the just penalty for such a crime. The desire for children was so great that in the early times a legitimate wife would agree to her husband's begetting them with one of her maids, as Abraham did, and Jacob after him."[2]

Additional Questions

- How would you describe the character of Zechariah and Elizabeth?
- Why do you think God chose Zechariah and Elizabeth to be John's parents?
- Do you think God gives people visions today like the one Zechariah had? Why, or why not?

AN ANGEL PROMISES THE BIRTH OF JESUS TO MARY
Luke 1:26-38

Additional Information

Luke probably talked with Mary personally before he wrote this account, which tells of her deep inward experiences, her calling, her fears, her submission, and her outburst of joy. Although Mary honestly confessed her feelings to God, she did not question His work in her life as Zechariah did. Her faith in God's sovereignty and the humility she demonstrated in accepting His plan is a powerful example to people today.

Additional Questions

- What were the main points of the angel's message?
- What do we learn about angels from this passage?
- What is significant about the fact that Jesus was born of a virgin?
- What does this passage reveal about Mary's character?
- What progressive changes do you see in Mary's attitude as she listened to the angel's message?

MARY VISITS ELIZABETH

Luke 1:39-56

Additional Information

Shortly after the angel's appearance, Mary spent three months visiting her relative Elizabeth. It isn't known whether Elizabeth was her aunt, cousin, or a more distant relative, but the bond between these two women went deeper than blood. God had chosen their family to welcome the Messiah into the world! Mary stayed with Elizabeth until John was born and then she returned to Nazareth.

Additional Questions

- What was the focus of the conversation between Mary and Elizabeth?
- What lessons have you learned from the experience of the two women that could be applied to your own relationships?
- Why are we often uncomfortable talking about God's work in our lives? When is this appropriate?

JOHN THE BAPTIST IS BORN

Luke 1:57-80

Additional Information

Because Zechariah and Elizabeth had been childless for such a long time, John's birth was an event of special joy for them. The Holy Spirit enabled Zechariah to prophesy concerning John's future, explaining that John would show Israel the way of salvation and forgiveness of sin. Zechariah's song also recognized the essential work of the coming Messiah.

John's parents, who were quite old at his birth, probably died when he was young. John grew up in the Desert of Judea, the area between Jerusalem and the Dead Sea. He didn't begin his public ministry until he was about thirty years old.

Additional Questions

- How would you summarize what Zechariah prophesied about Jesus (Luke 1:67-75)?
- What did Zechariah prophesy about John (Luke 1:76-79)?
- As you review this lesson, what principle or truth do you feel God wants you to apply to your life?
- What specific steps do you intend to take this week to apply these principles to your life?

NEXT TIME: News travels fast—especially when it's good news! In the next lesson, you'll see how the good news of Christ's birth spread and how people responded to it. The example of the shepherds and wise men will challenge you to renew your desire to worship and obey Jesus Christ.

LESSON THREE
A BLESSING FROM GOD

God chose the perfect time for the arrival of His Son, the promised Messiah, on earth.

> "[In] the world that cradled early Christianity, the 'fullness of the time' . . . [was] characterized by the following six features: (1) world centralization, (2) world cultural unity, (3) world trade and intercourse, (4) world peace (5) world demoralization, (6) world mingling of religions."[3]

OBJECTIVE: As a result of studying Jesus' birth, development, and childhood in this lesson, participants will be encouraged to renew their enthusiasm to live for Jesus.

Opening Questions

- What is it like to be around first-time parents?
- In what ways do we celebrate the birth of a child?

AN ANGEL APPEARS TO JOSEPH
Matthew 1:18-25

Additional Information

> "Betrothal with the ancient Hebrews was of a more formal and far more binding nature than the 'engagement' is with us. Indeed, it was esteemed a part of the transaction of

> marriage, and . . . the most binding part. . . . Among the Jews the betrothal was so far regarded as binding that, if marriage should not take place, owing to the absconding of the bridegroom or the breach of contract on his part, the young woman could not be married to another man until she was liberated by a due process and a paper of divorce. . . . The betrothed parties were legally in the position of a married couple, and unfaithfulness was 'adultery.'"[4]

Additional Questions

- Do you think the Jewish custom concerning engagement and divorce was a good one?
- Would it work today? Why, or why not?
- When have you discovered circumstances in your life have been divinely arranged to reveal or bring about God's will?
- How was God's sovereignty obvious?
- How can Scripture confirm our perception of God's leading?

JESUS IS BORN

Luke 2:1-20

Additional Information

In order to collect taxes effectively, the Romans required a census to be taken the year Jesus was born.

> "Had Judea been then, as in later days, a mere province, her census would have been taken after the Roman method, which enrolled the people wherever they chanced to reside; but since she was still a kingdom, it was taken after the Jewish method, which required each to repair to his ancestral seat and there report himself. Since Joseph was 'of the house and ancestry of David,' he must needs betake himself to Bethlehem, David's city, a three days' journey from Nazareth. And, notwithstanding her condition, he took Mary with him, not caring in the peculiar circumstances to leave her amid curious and ill-judging people."[5]

Additional Questions

- Why do you think the angels appeared to lowly shepherds rather than to some other class of people?
- What pattern of Christian service do you see in the behavior of the shepherds?

- How does the fact that Christ became a man and lived on earth meet the needs of humanity?
- How does this event meet the needs of your own heart?

MARY AND JOSEPH BRING JESUS TO THE TEMPLE

Luke 2:21-40

Additional Information

Like all Jewish male babies, Jesus was circumcised eight days after His birth. This was an ancient ritual of great significance to the Jewish people. But it was not a rite particular to them.

> "In the nations around [Israel] it marked admission to adult status in the tribe. But for Israel it was the outward sign of a relationship: God was to be their God; they were to be His people. It was a mark of ownership, and a reminder of the covenant 'between Me and you and your descendants after you' ([Genesis] 17:7)."[6]

Additional Questions

- What did Simeon prophesy about Jesus? About Mary (Luke 2:28-35)?
- What does the fact that Anna was a prophetess suggest to you?
- Can you identify with Anna in some way? If so, how?
- What lessons can we learn from Anna's life (Luke 2:36-38)?

VISITORS ARRIVE FROM EASTERN LANDS

Matthew 2:1-12

Additional Information

> "These men in all likelihood came from Persia, and had devoted their lives to the study of the stars. . . . Israel had been under Persian rule, and there is no doubt that the men of Persia had become acquainted with much of the religion and hope of the Hebrews; and they would in all likelihood be specially attracted by such predictions as coincided with their own religious habits. In all probability they knew the prophecy about the star out of Jacob, the scepter out of Judah. They knew that this star indicated the birth of a King,

> so that when they came they said, 'Where is He that is born King of the Jews, for we saw His star in the east, and are come to worship Him?'"[7]

The Magi sought this information from Herod, not knowing his evil reputation.

> "Herod's private life was unsavory, and characterized by cruelty. Over the years he killed two of his ten wives, at least three sons, a brother-in-law, and a wife's grandfather. When he himself was about to die, knowing that the people would rejoice at his demise, he commanded that the leading Jews be shut up in the arena at Jericho and be put to death when he expired. Thus he craftily planned that though there would be no mourning for his death, there would be mourning at his death. Fortunately, however, when the news of his death in 4 B.C. arrived, these prisoners were set free, and the passing of the tyrant was welcomed as a relief."[8]

Additional Questions

- Why do you think this account of the Gentile wise men is included in Scripture?
- Compare the visit of the wise men with the visit of the shepherds. What are the differences and the similarities?
- What was the first "gift" the wise men gave to Jesus? (It was not an object.)
- What personal conclusions and application can you draw from the lives and actions of the wise men?

THE ESCAPE TO EGYPT AND RETURN TO NAZARETH
Matthew 2:13-23

Additional Information

Whether the gifts of the wise men financed the escape of Joseph, Mary, and baby Jesus is not known, but for an undetermined period of time they remained in Egypt.

> "The nearest place of safety to which Joseph could flee with his family was Egypt. . . . Tradition says they penetrated more than a hundred miles within the country and abode for a year in a Jewish colony, in the village of Motorea near Leviantapolis, the site of a great Jewish Temple built in 150 B.C. There

> were more than a million Jews in Egypt at this time, and the colony was highly respectable and influential in the country. Thus the infant Savior was snatched from the savage fury of the wicked tyrant. Matthew found in this experience of Jesus the fulfillment of the prophecy [of Hosea]."[9]

The death of Herod in 4 B.C. signaled the return of Joseph and his family to Palestine. However, since Herod's cruel son Archelaus now reigned in Judea, God directed Joseph to withdraw to Nazareth in Galilee. Matthew views their return from Egypt as the fulfillment of the experiences of Israel (Hosea 11:1), and the settling in Nazareth as fulfilling the prophecy of Christ's lowly estate.

While Matthew doesn't mention Joseph's and Mary's trip to Jerusalem, Luke omits both the visit of the wise men and the flight into Egypt. These deletions are not contradictions, but natural results due to the specialized interests of the writers. You will encounter many similar gaps as you study the Gospels. Between the first and second portions of Luke 2:39 there is a time gap of a number of years. Do not let these time gaps confuse you. Instead, look for an explanation for any seeming contradiction, remembering that the whole body of Scripture is a single entity inspired by the Holy Spirit and thus consistent with itself.

Additional Questions

- What motivated Joseph to flee to Egypt with his family?
- Why did Joseph and his family visit and live in each of these places: Nazareth, Bethlehem, Jerusalem, and Egypt?

JESUS' YOUTH

Luke 2:41-52

Additional Information

Jesus' visit to the temple in Jerusalem "had a special significance, since the age of twelve marked His becoming bar-mitzvah, 'a son of the law.' At that point the Jewish boy reached the age of accountability and was formally inducted into the privileges and responsibilities of the community."[10]

Additional Questions

- What do you think constituted a major part of Jesus' education (Deuteronomy 6:4-9)?

▶What outstanding character traits are demonstrated by these people: Zechariah, Elizabeth, Joseph, Mary, the shepherds, the wise men, Simeon, and Anna?

▶Which trait impressed you the most?

▶How can you, by God's grace, develop this trait in your own life?

NEXT TIME: If the president or prime minister of your country told you he was coming to see you next week, you would probably go to great lengths to prepare for his visit. No doubt you would also call all of your friends and relatives to tell them he was coming. As you study the next lesson, you'll discover how John the Baptist prepared the world for Jesus. His example will inspire you to tell your friends about Christ's coming to earth.

THE BEGINNING

LESSON FOUR

INVITE A FRIEND!

> "The Messiah did not come unannounced. A coming king must have at least one attendant. It was customary for oriental monarchs to have a special herald to make way for them, but why should this apply to God's Messiah? Could not the heavens be suddenly opened and a heavenly voice announce to the world His mission? Such a method would have led men to think that His mission was designed to be spectacular. God chose otherwise; a human forerunner was selected. The herald's task was an honored one, and it would surely be expected that some notable person would be selected—yet God's choice fell on one among the lowly. The herald was to be born of humble stock."[11]

OBJECTIVE: As a result of this lesson, participants will learn how to follow John's example by inviting their friends to meet Jesus.

Opening Questions

- If you wanted to be an ambassador to another country, what qualifications do you think you would need?
- Why do we place such an emphasis on people's credentials?

JOHN THE BAPTIST PREPARES THE WAY FOR JESUS

Matthew 3:1-12, Mark 1:2-8, Luke 3:1-20, John 1:19-28

Additional Information

While Jesus awaited His time in the town of Nazareth, John lived in the desert until he appeared out of the wilderness boldly proclaiming a unique message of repentance. Descended from the priestly line of Aaron, John could have become a priest; but instead, God destined him to become the prophet of whom Malachi had written, "Behold, I am going to send My messenger, and he will clear the way before Me" (Malachi 3:1, NASB).

Additional Questions

- How would you describe John the Baptist's physical appearance (Matthew 3:4)?
- What was so significant about John the Baptist?
- What are some of the character traits you see in John?
- What did John teach the people to do (Luke 3:7-14)?
- How do you think you would have responded to John if you had seen and heard him?
- How would you summarize what John taught about Jesus?

JOHN BAPTIZES JESUS

Matthew 3:13-17, Mark 1:9-11, Luke 3:21-22, John 1:29-34

Additional Information

When God first gave the Law to Moses, He commanded that certain washings and purification ceremonies be followed. The act of baptism has as its roots Israel's ceremonial washing of their clothes in their consecration to receive the Law (Exodus 19:10-14) and in the preparation by washing of Aaron and his sons for their ordination to the priesthood (Leviticus 8:6). Other commands for ceremonial washing had to do with purification from defilement and disease (Leviticus 12–15).

Because the Pharisees carried the practice of ceremonial washing or baptism to excess without a genuine, inner change of heart, Jesus later severely rebuked them for their hypocrisy (see Matthew 23:25).

Additional Questions

- What did John's baptism normally indicate (Luke 3:3, see also Acts 19:4)?
- Why was John reluctant to baptize Jesus?
- What did John's baptism of Jesus indicate?
- What did the descending of the Holy Spirit on Jesus reveal?
- Why do you think God called a man like John for this unique ministry?

SATAN TEMPTS JESUS IN THE DESERT

Matthew 4:1-11, Mark 1:12-13, Luke 4:1-13

Additional Information

> "With this initial step of His public ministry, the whole plan and strategy of the messianic task must have been uppermost in the mind of Jesus. It is against such a background that the temptations that came to Him in the wilderness must be interpreted. They reflect something of His inner conflict throughout the forty days He spent alone. He did not even allow food to interrupt His meditations. Spiritual realities took precedence over physical needs. Those forty days became an intensive period of challenge. The intensity of the temptations almost certainly grew greater as physical strength declined."[12]

Additional Questions

- What declaration from God does the Devil call into question in two of the three temptations (Matthew 3:17, 4:3-6)?
- What false concept about God did Satan try to promote in each of these three temptations?
- Why did Jesus quote from Deuteronomy in each of His responses to the Devil?
- How did the Devil misuse Scripture (Psalm 91:11-12, Matthew 4:6)?
- What does this reveal about the Enemy?
- Why do you think this event and its timing are important?

THE FIRST DISCIPLES FOLLOW JESUS

John 1:35-51

Additional Information

When Jesus came out of the wilderness after the temptation, John pointed Him out as the One whose coming he had been announcing. Some of John's own disciples left him to follow Jesus. John had done his job well—he had prepared his disciples to recognize the Savior and encouraged them to follow Him. John's popularity never distracted him from his purpose to show people the way to the Messiah.

Additional Questions

- ▸Who took the initiative in the call of John and Andrew?
- ▸What implications might this fact have in soul-winning or discipleship today?
- ▸Why is it sometimes easier to witness to strangers than it is to our own family and friends?

NEXT TIME: Some of the funniest home videos take place at weddings. No matter how well the bride has planned the service and reception, something inevitably goes wrong—the groom faints, the cake topples over, or the bridesmaids end up arm wrestling over the brides' bouquet! The next lesson includes the story of a unique wedding feast in Cana of Galilee. An unexpected problem gave Jesus the opportunity to reveal His power.

THE BEGINNING

LESSON FIVE
IN THE PUBLIC EYE

After Jesus completed a time of testing in the desert, He began His public ministry. His time was at hand, and He began to reveal Himself to Israel as the promised Messiah. Christ's ministry took place during a three-year period that centered around four Passovers. He began His ministry during the first of these Passovers; in it He manifested Himself as the promised Messiah in the cleansing of the temple, which was His Father's house. He was crucified and rose again during the period of the fourth Passover. Between these two points in time (A.D. 27–30), He ministered publicly.

OBJECTIVE: As a result of this lesson, participants will understand how the early events in Jesus' ministry show that He is indeed the Son of God.

Opening Questions
- What do you enjoy most about attending a wedding?
- What is the funniest or strangest thing you've experienced at a wedding?

JESUS TURNS WATER INTO WINE
John 2:1-11

Additional Information
Three days after His conversation with Nathanael, Jesus, His mother, and His new followers attended a wedding feast in Cana of

Galilee. Here Jesus performed His first miracle.

During this wedding feast, the wine ran out and Jesus' mother presented the problem to her Son. (Wine used in Palestine during this time was mixed with three parts of water.) Jesus turned the water in the large jars into wine and the new wine was brought to the master of the banquet.

> "It was his duty of office to superintend the feast, examine and taste everything before it was served, see that all were served promptly, guide the conversation, repress undue excitement, and preserve order and decorum by breaking a glass when any guest might be disorderly, without naming him."[13]

After this spectacular, though private, miracle, Jesus and His family spent a few days in Capernaum, a city which would become His center of operations in the future. The time was now right for the beginning of His public ministry.

Additional Questions

- Why do you think Jesus was willing to change the water into wine at the wedding when He was unwilling to turn the stones into bread in the wilderness?
- How is Jesus shown to be the Son of God in this episode?
- How does this incident illustrate Christ's glory?
- Why do you think Christ chose to begin His ministry with such a quiet miracle in a small village in Galilee?

JESUS CLEARS THE TEMPLE

John 2:12-25

Additional Information

> "By the time Jesus had begun His public ministry the whole temple operation had become one huge system of graft. It had come into being under the ex-high priest Annas [before whom Jesus was later tried], who had established a market for the sale of sacrificial animals and a money exchange system in the temple.
>
> "The profession of money-changer in Palestine was made necessary by the law requiring every male Israelite who had reached the age of 20 years to pay into the treasury

of the sanctuary a half-shekel at every numbering of the people, an offering to Jehovah, not even the poor being exempt. It seems to have become an annual tax, and was to be paid in the regular Jewish half-shekel [Exodus 30:11-15]. Since the Jews, coming up to the feasts, would need to exchange the various coins in common circulation for this Jewish piece, there were moneychangers who exacted a premium for the exchange. . . . The Jews of Christ's day came from many parts of the world, and the business of exchanging foreign coins for various purposes became a lucrative one, the exchangers exacting whatever fee they might."[14]

"The animals for sacrifices and offerings had to be examined by persons qualified to do so and duly appointed. For such inspection there were exorbitant charges. Improper transactions were carried on and undue advantage taken. Sometimes a dove or lamb was sold for five or six times the just price. The whole traffic was a terrible desecration of religion. The profits were all supposed to flow into the Temple treasury; but the fact is that they went mainly to the moneychangers and to superintending priests to whom they in turn paid a percentage or rentals. This market in the time of Jesus was what Rabbinic literature called the 'Bazaars of the sons of Annas.' He was the infamous politician who dominated the High Priesthood for many years even after his deposition. These Bazaars were noted for the greed of their owners and were hated and feared by the common people."[15]

Additional Questions

- Why was Jesus angry at what seemed to be a legitimate and beneficial activity?
- What impact would driving the moneychangers and traders out of the temple have on the people? On the leaders?
- Why didn't the Jews stop Jesus?
- Considering the fact that our bodies are the "temple of the Holy Spirit," what kind of personal application can we make from this passage?
- To what extent should churches and pastors and religious groups engage in business?
- To what extent should the church be run like a business?

NICODEMUS VISITS JESUS AT NIGHT
John 3:1-21

Additional Information
Nicodemus was a member of the Sanhedrin, the ruling body of Judaism. He was probably a rich man, cultured, and in high social standing in the community. He came to Jesus to inquire about the Kingdom of God. John does not record where this conversation took place, but it could have been in his own Jerusalem home (see John 19:27).

Additional Questions
- Since the Pharisees believed in the Scriptures and in the resurrection of the dead, why were they so suspicious of Jesus?
- Why did Nicodemus think that Jesus was a teacher sent from God?
- Why did Nicodemus have trouble understanding what Jesus said?
- How does Jesus' message to Nicodemus, including the exposition in John 3:16-21, identify Jesus as the Son of God?
- What impact did the discussion with Jesus have on Nicodemus (see also John 7:43-53, 19:38-42)?
- What have you learned about eternal life from this passage?

JOHN THE BAPTIST TELLS MORE ABOUT JESUS
John 3:22-36

Additional Information
Some may wonder why John the Baptist didn't give up his ministry to follow Jesus. Even John's disciples weren't sure how to respond to Jesus—they loved John and had followed him faithfully, yet he had always told them to prepare themselves for the Messiah. John explained that Jesus was the one whose coming he had announced. Although Jesus had begun His public ministry, John continued to fulfill his role of pointing others to Him.

Additional Questions
- What implications concerning Christ's nature and authority do you see in the statement, "The Father loves the Son and has placed everything in his hands" (John 3:35)?
- Why do you think John continued his ministry after Christ became popular?

▶What does John say is the relationship of Christ to the Father?
▶What can we learn from John's attitude toward other potential "competitors" in the ministry?

NEXT TIME: The United States is known as a "melting pot." People from around the world think of this as the "land of opportunity." But being surrounded by different kinds of people doesn't mean that we automatically accept them. In the first lesson of *Challenging Tradition* in this series, you'll see how Jesus treated people who were despised and mistreated by others. His actions will challenge you to reevaluate your attitudes toward people who are different from you.

Challenging Tradition

CHALLENGING TRADITION

LESSON ONE
AN OBSTACLE COURSE

✣

"Yet not in Jerusalem and Judah will the light first dawn, but in the northernmost part of the land of Israel, a region which lay in darkness and death at the time Jesus came to fulfill the ancient prophecy, and which even John the Baptist had not been able to reach by his call to repentance."[1]

Jesus returned from His ministry in Jerusalem and traveled through Samaria to Galilee, the region where He was raised. The term Galilee, taken from the Hebrew word *galil*, means "circle." In this area, surrounded by non-Jewish people, Christ chose to begin His extensive ministry, traditionally called the Great Galilean Ministry.

OBJECTIVE: This lesson will challenge participants to identify things that weaken their Christian witness and will encourage them to begin eliminating those hindrances from their lives.

Opening Questions

- ▶Who is your best friend? What attracted you to that person?
- ▶What character traits do we usually look for in a friend? Why?

THE SAMARITAN WOMAN BELIEVES IN JESUS
John 4:1-42

Additional Information

Jesus started back to Galilee, taking the direct route through Samaria. For Jews to travel through Samaria was unusual, and

Jesus' conversation with the Samaritan woman was even more so.

Scripture says that it was about the sixth hour when Jesus arrived at the Well of Jacob in Sychar. The Jewish day began at sunrise, which was called the first hour; it ended at sunset, the twelfth hour; the sixth hour was always noon, the hottest time of the day.

Noon was an unusual time for a woman to be drawing water, and pointed out the fact that she was an outcast. Besides having serious moral problems (which Jesus uncovered), she was also well-versed in Samaritan religious beliefs and tried to divert the conversation to a theological discussion.

Additional Questions

- What do you think Jesus meant when He said that we are to worship God "in spirit and in truth" (John 4:23-24)?
- What principles did Jesus use in meeting this woman's spiritual needs?
- What does Jesus' analogy about food reveal about doing God's will (John 4:31-34)?
- What fears or prejudices prevent us from reaching out to certain people?
- What personal sacrifices do we sometimes have to make to share the gospel with others?

JESUS PREACHES IN GALILEE

Matthew 4:12, Mark 1:14-15, Luke 4:14-15, John 4:43-45

Additional Information

> "It was fitting that the ministry proper of Jesus should find its greatest expression in Galilee. It was the most beautiful, productive and populous district of Palestine. The bright sunny sea of Galilee with its sturdy fisher-folk, surrounded by a beautiful country, was a fit place, if there could be any, to serve as a setting for His wonderful life and activity. Galilee of the Gentiles was a choice cradle for the universal Gospel. Jesus liked to mingle in the crowd. He loved human beings and here He found a dense population made up of heterogeneous elements of all types and nationalities."[2]

Additional Questions

- How do you think Jesus felt about the people with whom He grew up?

▶How can we better prepare ourselves to answer our friends' questions about Jesus?

JESUS HEALS A GOVERNMENT OFFICIAL'S SON
John 4:46-54

Additional Information

Jesus visited Nazareth and other towns around Galilee before He returned to Cana, the place where He had turned the water into wine. While there He revealed His awesome power by healing a government official's son who was twenty miles away in Capernaum.

This miracle is recorded only in John's Gospel. John's purpose was to show that *all* who believe in Jesus will be saved. This story shows how Jesus treated a royal official who probably served Herod—He rewarded his simple faith with a miraculous demonstration of God's power.

Additional Questions

▶In what ways did the royal official demonstrate his faith in Jesus?

▶What was the result of this whole incident?

▶Do you think people who turn to God in physical or material desperation are likely to trust Him for salvation if He answers their request? Why, or why not?

▶What small step could you take today to demonstrate your faith in Jesus?

JESUS IS REJECTED AT NAZARETH
Luke 4:16-30

Additional Information

The news about Jesus spread throughout all of Galilee. For some time, He preached in the synagogues and was well received. But when He returned to His hometown of Nazareth, the people questioned His authority.

At the local synagogue, He quoted a passage describing the deliverance of Israel from her enemies and proclaimed that He was the one who would fulfill the prophecy (Isaiah 61:1-2). But God's plan of deliverance would be different than what the people expected. Israel wanted to be saved from the oppressive rule of the Roman empire, but Jesus came to save them from their sins.

His words of hope and freedom were warmly received, but

when Jesus compared the crowds' acceptance of the truth to the Israelites in the time of Elijah who were known for their wickedness, the people turned on Jesus.

Additional Questions

- Why do you think the Jews met primarily in synagogues at this time?
- What caused the people of Nazareth to be different from other Galileans and openly oppose Jesus?
- What explanation did Jesus give for their opposition?
- Why do people oppose Jesus today?
- How does Jesus' message illustrate that God reaches out to all people?

NEXT TIME: All children love to imitate—it's how they learn to function in the world. In fact, one of the scariest aspects of parenting is knowing that your children will copy everything you do and say! The next lesson will introduce you to the one person who *invites* you to imitate Him. Accepting His challenge will be the best decision you'll ever make!

CHALLENGING TRADITION

LESSON TWO
FOLLOW THE LEADER

"The expression 'Follow Me' would be readily understood, as implying a call to become the *permanent* disciples of a teacher. Similarly, it was not only the practice of the Rabbis, but regarded as one of the most sacred duties, for a Master to gather around him a circle of disciples. Thus, neither Peter and Andrew, nor the sons of Zebedee, could have misunderstood the call of Christ, or even regarded it as strange. . . .

"The call came *after* the open breach with, and initial persecution of, the Jewish authorities. It was, therefore, a call to fellowship in His peculiar relationship to the Synagogue. . . . It necessitated the abandonment of all their former occupations, and, indeed, of all earthly ties. . . . Such a call could [probably] not have been addressed to them, if they had not already been disciples of Jesus, understood His Mission, and the character of the Kingdom of God."[3]

OBJECTIVE: As a result of this lesson, participants will understand what it really means to follow Jesus Christ.

Opening Questions

- Who do you admire and respect as a leader? What makes that person a good leader?
- Why do we sometimes give up our own desires to help a leader accomplish his or her goals?

JESUS MOVES TO CAPERNAUM

Matthew 4:13-17, Luke 4:31

Additional Information

In his Gospel account, Matthew explains that Jesus' ministry fulfilled the prophecies of Isaiah, who predicted that the people in the "land of Zebulun and land of Naphtali" would see the Messiah (Isaiah 9:1-2). Jesus spent most of His public ministry in this area, which is north and west of the Sea of Galilee. Peter's house in Capernaum became Jesus' headquarters during His extensive ministry in Galilee. Capernaum had a synagogue and probably a Roman military garrison. It eventually became known as Jesus' city.

Additional Questions

- What was the significance of this move?
- Why does Isaiah refer to the area around Capernaum as a region of those who sit in "darkness" and in the "shadow of death" (Matthew 4:16)?
- Why does Matthew quote Isaiah here?
- How do you think God looks at churches today that resist His requirement for a radical change of attitude and lifestyle?

FOUR FISHERMEN FOLLOW JESUS

Matthew 4:18-22, Mark 1:16-20, Luke 5:1-11

Additional Information

> "The twelve arrived at their final intimate relation to Jesus only by degrees, three stages in the history of their fellowship with Him being distinguishable. In the first stage they were simply believers in Him as the Christ, and His occasional companions at convenient, particularly festive, seasons. . . .
>
> "In the second stage, fellowship with Christ assumed the form of an uninterrupted attendance on His person, involving entire, or at least habitual abandonment of secular occupations. . . .
>
> "The twelve entered on the last and highest stage of discipleship when they were chosen by their Master from the mass of His followers, and formed into a select band, to be trained for the great work of the apostleship."[4]

Additional Questions

- Why do you think Jesus called these four fishermen, out of so many other people, to discipleship at this time?
- What attracted these men to Christ?
- What are the implications of Jesus' challenge, "Follow Me and I will make you fishers of men"?
- What have you given up to follow Jesus?
- Do you think Jesus calls every Christian to this close walk with Him, or is His call limited to a few special people? Explain your answer.

JESUS HEALS AND TEACHES PEOPLE

Matthew 4:23-25; 8:1-4,14-17; 9:1-8; Mark 1:21–2:12; Luke 4:33-44; 5:12-26

Additional Information

Jesus healed people almost everywhere He went. After healing the sick, Jesus taught the people. The first three specific healings listed (Matthew 8:1-4,14-17; 9:1-8) took place while Jesus was still in Capernaum. He healed the leper and the paralytic after He had systematically set out to visit the towns and villages of Galilee (Mark 1:39). Once again, the Gospel writer reminds us that Jesus' actions fulfilled the words of the prophets, "He took up our infirmities and carried our sorrows" (Isaiah 53:4).

Additional Questions

- What does it mean "to teach with authority" (Mark 1:21-22)?
- Why do you think Jesus sometimes touched those He healed and other times only spoke?
- Why were the Pharisees so unsympathetic toward the sufferings of sick and oppressed people?
- What spiritual truths do you think are revealed by the healing of Peter's mother-in-law and her subsequent serving?

JESUS EATS WITH SINNERS AT MATTHEW'S HOUSE

Matthew 9:9-13, Mark 2:13-17, Luke 5:27-32

Additional Information

The extent to which Jesus stepped out of traditional Jewish attitudes toward sinners can only be understood in light of the rabbinical teachings of the times.

> "Rabbinism knew nothing of a forgiveness of sin, free and unconditional, unless in the case of those who had not the power of doing anything for their atonement. . . . Jesus Christ freely invited *all* sinners, whatever their past, assuring them of welcome and grace, the last word of Rabbinism is only despair, and a kind of Pessimism."[5]

Additional Questions

- Why were tax collectors despised by most Jews?
- What do we learn about Jesus from His attitude toward this man?
- Why do you think we are so concerned about personal appearances?
- What sometimes blinds us to the needs of people around us?

NEXT TIME: Chameleons have the unique ability to change their colors to match their surroundings. Because we all want to fit in and be accepted, it's tempting to act like a chameleon. In order to please or impress other people, we alter or hide our beliefs. The next lesson will reveal what Jesus thought about this kind of behavior.

CHALLENGING TRADITION

LESSON THREE
THE RIGHT ATTITUDE

At this period of His ministry, Jesus laid down a "platform of important principles for the enlightenment and guidance of His kingdom forces."

> "This sermon [the Sermon on the Mount] is not a mere ethical code but its sublime moral principles far surpass all human moral standards. Christ's idea of Righteousness as here set forth, became the kingdom's ideal of Righteousness which has never yet been approximately realized by humanity. In His universal eternal principles in this sermon, Jesus laid the basis for the kingdom work for all time. In one discourse, He superseded all previous standards and set up the new and final religious goal for the human race. He here uttered the final word about character and privilege, conduct and duty, religious ideals, the divine and human relations of men, and the supreme objective and goal in life and how to attain it."[6]

OBJECTIVE: As a result of this lesson, participants will be challenged to evaluate whether their attitudes line up with their actions.

Opening Questions

- In what circumstances do we often think it's acceptable to bend or break the rules?
- How do you feel when you see someone breaking the law and getting away with it?

RELIGIOUS LEADERS ASK JESUS ABOUT FASTING
Matthew 9:14-17, Mark 2:18-22, Luke 5:33-39

Additional Information
John's disciples objected to the fact that Jesus' disciples did not observe the traditional fasts with the pious Jews. Although the Law of Moses prescribed only one fast, that of the Day of Atonement (Leviticus 16:29-34), four other yearly fasts were practiced by the Jews after the Babylonian exile (Zechariah 7:5, 8:19). Jesus did not condemn fasting, but emphasized the importance of proper motives. He didn't want His disciples to follow the example of the Pharisees who fasted twice a week simply to impress others.

Additional Questions
- What point did Jesus make in His illustrations about the new and old garments and the new and old wineskins?
- How can we guard against the legalism of the Pharisees?
- Do you think fasting is a means to communicate with God in a way that would not be possible without fasting? Why, or why not?
- Is prayer always to be included with fasting? Explain your answer.

JESUS HEALS PEOPLE ON THE SABBATH
Matthew 12:1-21, Mark 2:23–3:12, Luke 6:1-11, John 5:1-47

Additional Information
Despite criticism from the religious leaders, Jesus continued to heal people on the Sabbath.

> "Apart from His claim to be the Messiah, there is no subject on which our Lord came into such sharp conflict with the religious leaders of the Jews as in the matter of Sabbath observance. He set Himself squarely against the current Rabbinic restrictions as contrary to the spirit of the original law of the Sabbath. The rabbis seemed to think that the Sabbath was an end in itself, an institution to which the pious Israelite must subject all his personal; . . . man might suffer hardship, but the institution must be preserved inviolate. . . . If there should arise a conflict between man's needs and the letter of the Law, man's higher interests and needs must take precedence over the law of the Sabbath."[7]

Additional Questions

- ▶Why did Jesus do these things on the Sabbath?
- ▶Why would the Pharisees have felt that it was permissible for the priests to work in the temple on the Sabbath, but it was not permissible to heal on the Sabbath?
- ▶What conclusions can you draw from Christ's encounter with the Pharisees?

JESUS SELECTS THE TWELVE DISCIPLES

Matthew 10:2-4, Mark 3:13-19, Luke 6:12-16

Additional Information

Selecting the twelve disciples was a critical event in Jesus' ministry, for these would be the men He would be working with; these men were to become disciple makers. There seems to be a contradiction in the names on the list of the apostles unless further research is done. Judas, the son of James, is called Thaddeus in Mark, and Lebbaeus in Matthew. Bartholomew is probably Nathanael. Peter stands first in all the lists and Judas Iscariot last. The names are usually arranged in pairs which may refer to their ministering together. The list contains two or three pairs of brothers and at least one pair of close friends—Philip and Nathanael. All except Judas Iscariot were Galileans; Judas was a Judean.

Additional Questions

- ▶What reasons, other than for prayer, might Jesus have had in retreating to the mountain?
- ▶What do Mark and Luke reveal about the selection of the Twelve?
- ▶Why do you think Jesus chose only twelve disciples?
- ▶What steps could you take to become a better minister for Christ?

JESUS GIVES THE BEATITUDES

Matthew 5:1-16, Luke 6:17-26

Additional Information

The exact location of this discourse is not known, but it is believed to have been somewhere between Capernaum and Gennesaret near the Sea of Galilee. Addressing His disciples and the crowds that followed Him, Jesus described the characteristics of those who belong in His Kingdom.

The Sermon on the Mount as recorded by Matthew was not a once-given teaching. Jesus probably gave the contents of this sermon many times during His ministry. Luke, for example, records a short sermon given on the plains (though the mount could have risen from the plains), which contains parts of the longer sermon written by Matthew. Throughout Jesus' ministry, however, many of the points are repeated in different forms and under different circumstances.

A beatitude is "a particular declaration of blessedness and especially of such a declaration coming from the lips of Jesus Christ."[8] These types of beatitudes occur frequently in the Old Testament, especially in the Psalms, and Jesus used beatitudes occasionally. "But apart from individual sayings of this type the name Beatitudes. . . . has been attached specifically to those words of blessing with which, according to both Matthew and Luke, Jesus began that great discourse which is known as the Sermon on the Mount."[9] When the word blessed is used with reference to man, it means favored or happy.

Additional Questions

- How is being "poor in spirit" related to humility?
- How can "mourning" produce happiness?
- How does this hunger and thirst for righteousness manifest itself in our lives?
- How do the beatitudes relate to Jesus' illustrations of salt and light?
- What qualities or activities can salt and light symbolize?

JESUS TEACHES ABOUT THE LAW

Matthew 5:17-48, Luke 6:27-36

Additional Information

Most of the Jews in this crowd had probably carefully studied all of the Old Testament prophecies about the Messiah, and now the words of the prophets were being fulfilled before their eyes. But Jesus' "preaching was so entirely different from that of the Pharisees and Sadducees (which was supposed to be based on the Old Testament), that the people were inclined to imagine His intention was to subvert the authority of God's Word and substitute His own in its place."[10]

Additional Questions

- How did Jesus describe His relationship to the Law?
- What do you think Jesus' statements about gouging out a sinful eye and cutting off a sinful hand mean for us today?
- Why do you think Jesus instructed His disciples not to swear at all?
- How can a Christian today obey this command?
- In light of these six specific commandments, what general principle should govern our relationships with others in our families, churches, and communities?
- In what area of your life do you need to realign your attitudes and actions?

NEXT TIME: "Beauty is in the eye of the beholder." In the next lesson, we'll learn that this well-known saying applies to the Christian life. While the world pressures us to do whatever it takes to look our best physically, Jesus tells us that God cares much more about inner beauty. When we allow Christ to work in our hearts, He makes us beautiful in God's sight.

LESSON FOUR
WHAT A DIFFERENCE!

Although Matthew includes the Lord's Prayer at this point in his Gospel (Matthew 6:9-13), Luke records it later (Luke 11:2-4). We will study the Lord's Prayer in *Following Jesus* lesson 4. You may want to mention to group members that it will be covered in that lesson.

OBJECTIVE: This lesson will introduce participants to people whose lives were drastically changed when they met Jesus. These stories will challenge them to open their hearts and lives to Christ's convicting work.

Opening Questions

- What drastic steps do some people take to improve their outward appearance?
- Why do you think it's so easy to become obsessed with looking younger and more beautiful?
- Who is one person you admire for his or her inner beauty?

JESUS TEACHES ABOUT GIVING AND PRAYER
Matthew 6:1-8, 6:16–7:12; Luke 6:37-42

Additional Information

Having defined the relationship of His teachings to the Law, Jesus explained the motives and principles of conduct that apply to religious and social duties. A common theme of Jesus' teaching emerges again in this passage—the dangers of hypocrisy. Jesus told His followers to do good, not to gain praise and honor from others, but out of love for God and a genuine desire to serve others. He also condemned the empty practices of many of the religious leaders, warning His disciples to avoid their behavior. We need to remember that God focuses on the quality of our deeds, not the quantity.

Additional Questions

- What three things did Jesus say to do in secret? Why (Matthew 6:1-18)?
- According to Jesus, what are the advantages of keeping quiet about spiritual disciplines?
- What should be our primary concern? Why (6:33)?
- Why is it tempting to publicize our good deeds?
- How would you define "judging" as it is used in this context?
- Why shouldn't we judge others (7:1-6)?
- How would you summarize what Jesus promised His followers (7:7-12)?
- When we give money to the church or help a person in need, how can we know whether our motives are pure?
- How can you remind yourself to check your motives the next time you pray, give, or help?

JESUS TEACHES ABOUT THE WAY TO HEAVEN

Matthew 7:13-29, Luke 6:43-49

Additional Information

The crux of the gospel message is revealed in this passage—the only way to enjoy eternal life is to have a relationship with Jesus Christ. He alone offers us forgiveness from sin and a restored relationship with the Father. Jesus warns us to watch out for people who try to distort this truth. We can recognize these false teachers by studying their lives—a person who consistently exhibits sinful attitudes and immoral behavior probably does not have a genuine relationship with Jesus Christ.

Additional Questions

- How would you distinguish between good and bad fruit?
- What application can we make of this section on good and bad fruit to life in the Christian community (Matthew 7:15-23)?

- How does the world pressure or entice us to follow the crowd down the wrong road?
- How do you plan to protect yourself from the world's pressures and distractions?

A ROMAN CENTURION DEMONSTRATES FAITH
Matthew 8:5-13, Luke 7:1-10

Additional Information
Following the Sermon on the Mount, Jesus returned to the fishing village of Capernaum, which He had made His home. But again privacy and rest eluded Him, since many people came to Him to have their physical and spiritual needs met. Jesus astonished His listeners with both the content of His teaching and the authority with which He spoke. As He walked down from the Mount, a great crowd of people followed Him. When He entered Capernaum, the representative of a Roman centurion approached Him. While the Jews hated most Gentiles, the people of Capernaum loved this centurion because of his many good deeds in the community.

Additional Questions
- Why would a Roman soldier be kind to Jews?
- What is the relationship between faith and humility as demonstrated by the centurion?
- How did Jesus use this example of faith to teach the multitudes?
- Why does faith in Jesus Christ require humility?

JESUS RAISES A WIDOW'S SON FROM THE DEAD
Luke 7:11-17

Additional Information

> "Certain procedures were practiced at Jewish funerals that were in marked contrast to the approach of Jesus. Mourners were hired to chant a lament. This was designed not as a comfort to the bereaved, but as a measure of the respect in which the dead person was held. There was little attempt to relieve the sorrow."[11]

Additional Questions

- ▸How did Jesus respond to the situation He encountered in Nain?
- ▸How do you think the widow's life was changed as a result of Jesus' miracle?
- ▸In what specific ways has your relationship with Jesus changed you?
- ▸How does this miracle represent spiritual regeneration?

NEXT TIME: Marriage is more than the joining of two lives, it is the merging of two families. When you agree to marry a person, you also agree to become a member of his or her family. In the same way, when you commit your life to Jesus Christ, you become part of His family. As you study the next lesson, you will discover both the benefits and responsibilities involved in joining the family of God.

LESSON FIVE
THE FAMILY OF GOD

In Luke 8:1-3, the Gospel writer explains that several women accompanied Jesus and His disciples on a preaching trip through Galilee. Touched by Jesus' ministry, these women now traveled with Him and the crowds, providing money for His needs along the way. In this lesson, we will study the actions of one of these women who had probably left a life of prostitution to follow Jesus. The way He treated her will reveal the depth of His forgiveness and His desire for *all* to be saved.

OBJECTIVE: As a result of this lesson, participants will gain a better understanding of Christ's forgiveness and will be challenged to follow His example by welcoming all people into God's family.

Opening Questions

- What are some of the challenges and pressures families face today?
- In your opinion, what keeps a family together?

JESUS EASES JOHN'S DOUBT

Matthew 11:1-30, Luke 7:18-35

Additional Information

John the Baptist wasn't a weak person who easily succumbed to peer pressure, yet he was confused about what to believe. While in prison, he relied on his followers to keep him informed. Their reports of Jesus' activities made John wonder whether Jesus was indeed the One they had been waiting for. Jesus' work wasn't bringing the results that he expected from the Messiah.

Jesus responded patiently to John's discouragement and doubt. Rather than offering him empty promises, He told John's disciples to give him the hard facts. He pointed to the impressive miracles He had performed and, more importantly, His consistent message of salvation. Jesus knew that comparing His ministry to the Old Testament prophecies about the Messiah would reveal the truth about His identity (Isaiah 29:18-21, 35:5-6, 61:1; see also Luke 4:18).

Additional Questions

▶What kind of a person was Herod?
▶According to this passage, how does Jesus want us to deal with doubt?
▶What do you think is the yoke and burden of Jesus (Matthew 11:29-30)?
▶How do we take Jesus' yoke?
▶Is this a once-for-all taking of Christ's burden and yoke, or is it something we do continually?

A SINFUL WOMAN ANOINTS JESUS' FEET

Luke 7:36–8:3

Additional Information

Jesus, invited to a Pharisee's house to eat, was approached by a sinful woman while He was reclining at the table. Scholars tell us, "This woman was neither Mary of Bethany (John 12:1-8) nor Mary Magdalene. She was an unchaste woman (verse 37), a prostitute likely converted under John's or Jesus' ministry. . . . The Oriental banquet was in a Pharisee's house. Guests reclined, so it was easy for the woman to wash Jesus' feet with her tears and anoint them."[12]

Additional Questions

▶Why do you think the Pharisee reacted as he did to the woman's anointing Jesus?
▶What was Jesus' reaction to her anointing Him?
▶What was Jesus teaching Simon in this incident?
▶In what ways are Christians sometimes like the Pharisee in this story?
▶In light of Jesus' example, how should we treat the less fortunate people around us?

▶Who is one person you would like to treat differently because of what you have learned from this passage?

RELIGIOUS LEADERS FALSELY ACCUSE JESUS

Matthew 12:22-45, Mark 3:20-30, Luke 11:14-28

Additional Information

Though the New Testament says very little about the origin, nature, characteristics, or ways of demons, they are a present reality. In Scripture, the demon is an ethically evil being who belongs to the kingdom of Satan, or Beelzebub, and opposes God and His plans. As Jesus ministered to the people, a blind and dumb demon-possessed man was brought to Him. Jesus healed the man which once again brought more accusations from the religious leaders.

Additional Questions

▶What must have been in the minds of the Jewish leaders that prompted them to make this blasphemous accusation?

▶What is the significance of Jesus' answer to the scribes and Pharisees after they demanded a sign from Him (Matthew 12:38-45)?

▶What is blasphemy against the Holy Spirit? Why can it not be forgiven?

▶Why was it easier for Nineveh to repent than for the Jewish leaders to accept Jesus (Matthew 12:41)?

JESUS DESCRIBES HIS TRUE FAMILY

Matthew 12:46-50, Mark 3:31-35, Luke 8:19-21

Additional Information

Jesus had four brothers and at least two sisters (Matthew 13:55-56); Joseph was probably dead, and the family was now living in Capernaum where Jesus had moved them.

> "These brothers were friendly toward Jesus earlier in His ministry (John 2:12); but after He was rejected in Nazareth (Luke 4:16-31) there seems to have developed in them a disbelief as to His claims; and later on they ridiculed Him, calling Him the 'Secret Messiah' (John 7:5). At the present juncture they were unbelieving and indifferent, not to say hostile, or at least ready to interfere with His work in favor of a kind of quiet and respectable life for the family."[13]

Interestingly, two of Jesus' brothers would later write New Testament books—James and Jude.

Additional Questions

- What did Jesus mean by His response concerning His family?
- Why are spiritual ties between people often closer than family ties?
- Why do you think it is so important for believers to get along?

NEXT TIME: It's fun to imagine what it would be like to be a prince or princess. As believers, however, we need to remember that we are heirs to a Kingdom much bigger and better than any earthly kingdom. The first lesson of *The Messiah* in this series will introduce you to the King and show you how the Kingdom is run.

The Messiah

THE MESSIAH

LESSON ONE
KING OF KINGS

✣

Because of the opposition Jesus was now encountering from the religious leaders, He began teaching by parables. These stories used common experiences to reveal important spiritual truths. The religious leaders were more interested in criticizing Jesus than in trying to learn from Him, so they usually missed the message of His parables. You will see in this lesson that Jesus' own followers didn't always understand what He was trying to communicate in these short stories, so He had to explain them to His disciples privately.

OBJECTIVE: As a result of this lesson, participants will gain a better understanding of the values, rules, and priorities in God's Kingdom.

Opening Questions

▶What major changes have you experienced in the past five years?
▶What aspects of your life have stayed the same?
▶Why do you think we often resist change?

....

JESUS TEACHES THROUGH PARABLES

Matthew 13:1-52, Mark 4:1-34, Luke 8:4-18

Additional Information

Enthusiastic crowds still followed Jesus, so He climbed into a boat, and taught them as they sat on the shore of the Sea of Galilee. He told the parables of the growing seed and the mustard seed to reveal important truths of the Kingdom of God.

Additional Questions

- According to the parable of the sower, what keeps people from hearing and obeying God's Word?
- What happens when we hear and accept the truth of Christ's message?
- What does the parable of the growing seed teach us about the process of maturing in Christ?
- How does the parable of the net and fish (Matthew 13:47-52) relate to the parable of the good and bad seed growing together?
- How has your sensitivity to God's Word been dulled by the worries of life, the appeal of wealth, and other worldly temptations?
- In what area of your life do you need to allow God's Word to make a real difference?

JESUS CALMS THE STORM

Matthew 8:23-27, Mark 4:35-41, Luke 8:22-25

Additional Information

After the events of the preceding day, the disciples were profoundly impressed.

> "Here was one who in the same day had cured a blind-dumb lunatic, met the learned Scribes and Pharisees in debate and defeated them, taught many wonderful things in beautiful but half-enigmatic parables, and [then] with a word [made] the cyclonic winds cease and [calmed] the raging sea. They were filled with amazement. . . .
>
> "They were growing in their apprehension and comprehension of Jesus, but they had much to learn yet and needed to grow in the knowledge of the Lord Jesus Christ. At least they had caught one more glimpse of His majesty and were filled with dread and wonder. He was not just the human Jesus then; He was also the divine Christ."[1]

Additional Questions

- If you had been one of the disciples, how do you think you would have felt and reacted throughout this experience?
- In your opinion, what are the most interesting aspects of this incident?
- How does Jesus want us to handle life's storms?

JESUS SENDS THE DEMONS INTO A HERD OF PIGS

Matthew 8:28-34, Mark 5:1-20, Luke 8:26-39

Additional Information

Jesus led His band of disciples into the non-Jewish territory of the Decapolis. They reached the eastern side of the Sea of Galilee near Gergasa.

> "Suddenly, weird terrifying shrieks rent the night air. Darting from behind the tombs, two demoniacs swiftly bore down on the little group. One of them was notorious and utterly uncontrollable. Men had tried using chains to tame him, but he shattered the links to pieces. His frenzied strength was phenomenal, and no one dared to pass where he lived. The disciples must have been terrified. . . . Or had their faith grown stronger since the stilling of the storm? . . . Surely the disciples were also overawed by the dignity and authority of Jesus as He stood facing the advancing demoniacs.
>
> "Mark and Luke concentrate on the more notorious demoniac, but Matthew includes them both. There are other stories where Matthew included two and the other writers mentioned only one (e.g., two blind men at Jericho; two asses at the entry into Jerusalem)."[2]

Additional Questions

- ▶How would you describe the demon-possessed man before and after Jesus dealt with him?
- ▶How would you describe your life before and after you met Jesus Christ?
- ▶Why do you think Jesus did not take the former demoniac with Him?
- ▶Why is it sometimes more difficult to serve Christ at home than in a strange place?
- ▶Which of your goals or plans is hindering God's work in your life?

JESUS HEALS PEOPLE AND RAISES A GIRL TO LIFE

Matthew 9:18-34, Mark 5:21-43, Luke 8:40-56

Additional Information

The supervisors who controlled services in the synagogues were known as rulers. Their duties included the selection of who was to read from the Law and the Prophets and who was to preach. They also led discussions and generally kept order. Jairus, one of these rulers, approached Jesus because his only daughter was dying.

While Jesus was on the way to Jairus's home, a woman touched the edge of His cloak—her faith in His healing power changed her instantly. Unlike the countless people who surrounded Jesus to satisfy their curiosity, this woman desperately wanted to be healed by Him. Her faith made the difference! Jesus works in the same way today. We may claim to know God and see how He has changed other people, but we won't personally experience His power until we put our faith in Him.

Additional Questions

- Why did Jesus ask who had touched Him?
- When have you seen clear evidence of God's power?
- How was your life affected?

NEXT TIME: Money, power, comfort, status, excitement, recognition—the world tells us we can have it all! But the next lesson will show us the price tag that's attached to all these "good things." We will learn that, in light of eternity, giving up the world's pleasures to obey Christ is worth it. The best things in this world pale in comparison to the joy of Heaven!

LESSON TWO

IT'S WORTH IT!

Jesus' ministry schedule was grueling! Every time He entered a new town, sick and diseased people surrounded Him, begging for mercy. Religious leaders relentlessly criticized Him, accusing Him of disobeying their rules and regulations. Even Jesus' own disciples needed His constant attention. But despite overwhelming physical and spiritual needs, Jesus continued traveling from town to town, healing people and sharing the gospel message. Jesus understood His God-given role and willingly gave up His own needs and desires to fulfill His mission.

OBJECTIVE: As a result of this lesson, participants will gain a better understanding of the cost involved in following Christ. They will also learn that the eternal benefits of standing firm in the faith are worth the temporary sacrifices.

Opening Questions

- What is your favorite television commercial? Why?
- How do advertisers try to convince us to purchase their products?
- Why do you think so many people believe that material things can bring happiness and fulfillment?

THE PEOPLE OF NAZARETH REFUSE TO BELIEVE

Matthew 13:53-58, Mark 6:1-6

Additional Information

After Jesus raised Jairus's daughter from the dead, He healed two blind men and cured a demoniac (Matthew 9:27-34). Then He paid

His last recorded visit to Nazareth. When the people in His hometown heard Jesus preaching in the synagogue, they questioned His authority. They couldn't believe that a carpenter's son could grow up to be such a wise teacher. They saw Him as Joseph's son, not the Son of God. Jesus was amazed at their lack of faith and refused to perform many miracles there because of their pride and unbelief. Jesus explained that prophets are often despised by their own families and relatives. The prophet Jeremiah was rejected by the people in his hometown, and his own family betrayed him (Jeremiah 12:5-6).

As Christians, we will all experience criticism for obeying God. But we can't allow fear of rejection to keep us from doing the Lord's work. God can still use us, even when others don't recognize the value of our service.

Additional Questions

- What is the tone of the people's statements about Jesus?
- What deep need in their lives did their sarcastic rejection of Jesus mask?
- What happened as a result of the Nazarene's lack of faith?
- Do you think Jesus' miracles are limited by our lack of faith? Why, or why not?
- What concrete action can you take to strengthen your faith in Jesus Christ?

JESUS SENDS OUT THE TWELVE DISCIPLES

Matthew 9:35–10:42, Mark 6:7-13, Luke 9:1-6

Additional Information

Jesus' sending out of the twelve disciples shows us how we are to live for Him in the world today. It is important for us to realize that our commitment to God will clash with the people around us who have rejected Him. They may criticize or persecute us when we try to share the gospel with them. But Jesus encourages us to stand firm in our faith, even in the face of opposition. The key is to rely on His strength, not our own.

After receiving their instructions, the disciples went out as Jesus had commanded them (Mark 6:12, Luke 9:6). Jesus Himself continued teaching and preaching in the villages of Galilee (Matthew 11:1).

Additional Questions

- What do you think Jesus meant when He said, "Whoever loses his life for my sake will find it"?
- Why were the disciples forbidden to go to the Gentiles and the Samaritans?
- Was their message the same as the "Great Commission" Christ gave them after His resurrection to "preach the good news to all creation"?
- Why do you think it was or was not the same?
- When have you been mistreated or criticized because of your relationship with Jesus? How did you feel?

HEROD KILLS JOHN THE BAPTIST

Matthew 14:1-12, Mark 6:14-29, Luke 9:7-9

Additional Information

When Herod the Great died, Palestine was divided into four territories and given to four of his sons. Herod, also known as Herod Antipas, ruled over the regions of Galilee and Perea. Herod's half brother Philip ruled over the territory northeast of the Sea of Galilee. Herodias, a granddaughter of Herod the Great, first married her uncle, Philip, and then left him to marry Herod Antipas. This union was forbidden by Old Testament Law (Leviticus 18:16), so John the Baptist publicly condemned their immoral lifestyle. Eventually, Herodias devised a plan to convince Herod to have John the Baptist beheaded. (Up to this point, John had been imprisoned nearly a year in the dungeon called Machaerus, east of the Dead Sea.)

Additional Questions

- Why was John in prison?
- Why was he killed?
- How do Herod's actions (Mark 6:17-29) compare to each of the three areas of sin listed in 1 John 2:15-16?
- How does the life story of John the Baptist challenge you to change?
- What keeps many Christians from sharing their faith with others?
- When has your desire to please people hindered your Christian witness?

JESUS FEEDS THE FIVE THOUSAND

Matthew 14:13-21, Mark 6:30-44, Luke 9:10-17, John 6:1-15

Additional Information

When the twelve apostles returned from the mission on which Jesus had sent them, they told Jesus about their experiences while ministering in the cities of Galilee (Luke 9:10). Perhaps, as part of the training of His men, Jesus wanted to evaluate the results of their mission. In search of a solitary place for fellowship and recuperation, they got into a boat and crossed the Sea of Galilee. But instead of finding a quiet place, they discovered the crowds had followed them. Jesus had compassion on the people and ministered to their physical and spiritual needs.

Additional Questions

- Why did Jesus ask the disciples for advice?
- If you had to write a brief newspaper article about this incident as if you had actually been a reporter witnessing the event, what would it say?
- What headline would you choose?
- What personal rights or needs do we sometimes have to sacrifice in order to please God?
- How can we serve God wholeheartedly and at the same time prevent ourselves from burning out?
- In what practical way can you show Christ-like compassion to a friend this week?

NEXT TIME: Everyone loves a good mystery—compiling the facts of the case, studying the evidence, and eliminating suspects is all part of the fun. The challenge of the next lesson is to gather all the facts about Jesus of Nazareth to determine His real identity. As you take a closer look at His words and actions, you will discover the truth about Jesus.

THE MESSIAH

LESSON THREE

SOLVE A MYSTERY...

✣

By this time Jesus had become well-known throughout Palestine and the surrounding areas. Although He was popular with the crowds, the religious leaders hated Him and created controversy whenever they could. As you study this lesson, look for reasons why the crowds were drawn to Jesus and for causes of the rising tensions between the Pharisees and Jesus.

OBJECTIVE: As a result of this lesson, participants will better understand how Jesus' words and actions prove that He is the Son of God.

Opening Questions

▸In what ways do we show our friends that they can trust us?

▸Why do you think some people find it hard to trust others?

JESUS WALKS ON WATER

Matthew 14:22-36, Mark 6:45-56, John 6:16-21

Additional Information

The feeding of the five thousand brought such a response from the crowds that they were ready to take Jesus and force Him to be king. Later that evening, Jesus went into the hills alone to pray and ordered His disciples to return to Bethsaida, on the other side of the sea. But due to a strong wind which had come up against them, the disciples had, by three o'clock in the morning, sailed no more than three or four miles.

Additional Questions

- What do Matthew 14:22-36 and John 6:16-21 add to the account given in Mark's Gospel?
- What lessons do you think Jesus was trying to teach His disciples?
- Why do you think we often doubt God's presence or His ability to help us?

JESUS IS THE TRUE BREAD FROM HEAVEN
John 6:22-71

Additional Information

After calming the storm and the disciples' hearts, Jesus and His men reached the eastern shore at Gennesaret. Here He healed many people. The next day, Jesus and the disciples sailed across the lake to Capernaum, where He was again confronted by large crowds. He challenged their devotion in His discourse on the bread of life.

Additional Questions

- What condition for having eternal life is laid down in John 6:40?
- Are there any other conditions we must meet in order to have eternal life? Why, or why not?
- What did Jesus teach about Himself in this discourse?
- What did Jesus mean when He referred to eating His flesh and drinking His blood?
- What caused many of the disciples to turn away from Jesus, as we see in John 6:66?
- Why did Jesus make it so difficult to be a disciple?

JESUS TEACHES ABOUT INNER PURITY
Matthew 15:1-20, Mark 7:1-23

Additional Information

Evidently Jesus' ministry had caused a stir as far away as Jerusalem, for some Jewish leaders made the trip from the capital to Galilee to question Him. Their goal was not to seek the truth, but to try to discover a discrepancy in Jesus' teaching or lifestyle. Above all, they wanted to discredit Jesus in front of the crowds; instead, Jesus exposed their hypocrisy.

> "Whatever was most spiritual, living, human and grand in the Scriptures they [the Pharisees] passed by. Generation

> after generation the commentaries of their famous men multiplied, and the pupils studied the commentaries instead of the text. Moreover, it was a rule with them that the correct interpretation of a passage was as authoritative as the text itself; and, the interpretations of the famous masters being as a matter of course believed to be correct, the mass of opinions which were held to be as precious as the Bible itself grew to enormous proportions. These were 'the traditions of the elders.'"[3]

Jesus confronted the Pharisees about their practice of Corban to reveal their twisted thinking.

> "[Corban] is the most general term for a sacrifice of any kind. In the course of time it became associated with an objectionable practice. Anything dedicated to the temple by pronouncing the votive word Corban forthwith belonged to the temple, but only ideally; actually it might remain in the possession of him who made the vow. So a son might be justified in not supporting his old parents simply because he designated his property or a part of it as a gift to the temple, that is, as [Corban]. There was no necessity for fulfilling his vow, yet he was actually prohibited from ever using his property for the support of his parents."[4]

Additional Questions

- ▶Why wasn't Jesus concerned that His disciples observe the tradition of washing their hands?
- ▶What is the difference between a commandment of God and tradition?
- ▶What was wrong with the Pharisees' attitude?
- ▶How would you define legalism?
- ▶How can we detect a legalistic attitude in our own lives?
- ▶How can we evaluate our convictions and practices to see whether they spring from the tradition of men or from the Word of God?

JESUS SENDS A DEMON OUT OF A GIRL

Matthew 15:21-28, Mark 7:24-30

Additional Information

Jesus at this time withdrew to Tyre and Sidon. This territory and its major centers, immediately north of Galilee, were coastal cities of

Phoenicia and a part of the Roman province of Syria. In this Gentile territory a pagan woman came to Jesus.

> "She was a Grecian from the district of Syro-Phoenicia. She had a young daughter possessed by demons. Reports of Jesus had spread as far as Tyre and Sidon (cf. Mark 3:8). The woman had probably decided what she would do if Jesus ever came into her vicinity. The main feature of the narrative concerns her meeting with Jesus and begging Him to do something. Matthew gives her urgent plea, 'Have mercy on me, O Lord, Son of David; my daughter is severely possessed by a demon.' It is strange that a Gentile should use the title 'Son of David,' but she obviously knew something about Jewish affairs."[5]

Additional Questions

- Why did Jesus twice refuse the woman's request for help?
- What is revealed about the attitudes of the woman, the disciples, and Jesus?
- Why do you think the disciples were so intolerant of this woman?
- What lessons can we learn from the Canaanite woman?

JESUS FEEDS FOUR THOUSAND

Matthew 15:29-39, Mark 7:31–8:10

Additional Information

> "How long Jesus and His apostles remained in the borders of Tyre is unknown. Possibly the fame of the miracle forced Him to leave sooner than He had proposed. He did not return south to Capernaum, but took His way in a north-easterly direction, up through the region of Sidon. He likely followed the caravan road from the region of Sidon on the south side of the river Bostrenus, crossing a lofty spur of the Lebanon range amidst peaks six thousand feet high, and passed over the natural rock-bridge spanning the Leontes (River). . . .
>
> "His destination was further to the south, in the borders of Decapolis, the territory of the ten allied Greek free cities."[6]

Additional Questions

- ▶What are the differences and similarities between the feeding of the four thousand and the feeding of the five thousand (see John 6:3-14)?
- ▶Why do you think Jesus involved the disciples in the feeding of the four thousand?
- ▶What demonstration of God's power in your past encourages you to trust Him with your future?
- ▶For what problem or difficulty in your life do you need to trust Christ today?

NEXT TIME: God has given all of us free will—this means that we have the freedom to reject His offer of salvation or accept it. This decision is the most important we will ever make because it determines how we will spend eternity. The next lesson will give you a better understanding of the costs of accepting Christ and the costs of rejecting Him.

LESSON FOUR
A LIFE-CHANGING DECISION

Jesus and His disciples traveled a roundabout way from Tyre and Sidon back to Galilee through the Ten Cities. On His way to Caesarea Philippi from the Decapolis, Jesus stopped at Magdala (also Magadon and Dalmanutha) where the Jewish leaders questioned His authority. When He arrived in Caesarea Philippi, He used a discussion with religious leaders to teach His disciples about upcoming events.

OBJECTIVE: As a result of this lesson, participants will better understand the benefits of accepting Christ's call and the consequences of rejecting Him.

Opening Questions

▶When have you had a hard time making up your mind about something?

▶What are some of the consequences of indecision?

RELIGIOUS LEADERS ASK FOR A SIGN IN THE SKY

Matthew 16:1-12, Mark 8:11-21

Additional Information

The leaven used in biblical times served the same function as yeast does today. A small lump of dough called leaven was saved from every batch. The next time dough was made this small lump was used to make it rise; then a new lump was saved for the next baking. When Jesus heard the disciples talking about their need for more bread to eat, Jesus compared yeast to the evil of the religious leaders. In the same way that a small lump of yeast can make a whole batch of bread rise, the stubborn unbelief of the religious leaders would soon contaminate the whole community and cause it to rise up against Jesus Christ.

Additional Questions

- What did Jesus mean by the "signs of the times" (Matthew 16:3)?
- Why did Jesus compare the teaching of the Pharisees and Sadducees to leaven?
- Why were the disciples so slow to comprehend the spiritual content of Jesus' teaching?
- How is this sometimes true for us?
- What are some practical ways we can be on our guard against legalism and secularism?
- What excuses do we use to get out of doing what God wants?

JESUS RESTORES SIGHT TO A BLIND MAN

Mark 8:22-26

Additional Information

Similar to the healing described in this passage, the spiritual healing Jesus does in our lives is a gradual process. He reveals spiritual truth to us slowly, as we put our faith in Him. When you feel discouraged about your spiritual progress, wait patiently before the Lord, remembering who Jesus is and His power to help in times of need.

Additional Questions

- Why do you think the townspeople begged Jesus to touch this blind man?
- Why, in your opinion, was the man told not to tell others?
- Why do you think Jesus healed people in so many different ways?
- Why do we often find it difficult to wait for God to act?
- What inhibits or slows down our spiritual progress?

PETER SAYS JESUS IS THE MESSIAH

Matthew 16:13-20, Mark 8:27-30, Luke 9:18-20

Additional Information

From this point on, the emphasis of Jesus' ministry changes distinctly.

"The day at Caesarea Philippi marks the watershed of the Gospels. From this point onwards, the streams begin to flow in another direction. The current of popularity which seemed likely in the earlier days of Jesus' ministry to carry Him to the throne has now been left behind. The tide sets toward the cross. The Galilean sunshine is suddenly clouded over, and the air grows sultry and heavy with the gathering storm. The voices shouting applause die away, and another more ominous note is heard. At Caesarea Jesus stood, as it were, on a dividing-line. It was like a hilltop from which He could see behind Him all the road He had traveled, and in front of Him the dark, forbidding way awaiting Him. One look He cast back to where the afterglow of happy days still lingered, and then faced around and marched forward towards the shadows. His course was now set to Calvary."[7]

Additional Questions

- In your own words, what is the church?
- How does Jesus' statement in Matthew 16:17 throw light on the reason why some people reject the deity of Christ?
- What kind of confidence can we have in our ministry as a result of Jesus' words (Matthew 16:17-19)?
- How does the world pressure us to deny Christ's true identity?

JESUS PREDICTS HIS DEATH THE FIRST TIME

Matthew 16:21-28, Mark 8:31–9:1, Luke 9:21-27

Additional Information

Peter's declaration that Jesus was the Christ represented the conviction of the other disciples. This confession of faith opened the door to a new depth in Jesus' teaching. He began to reveal to the disciples what being the Messiah really meant and what was going to happen to Him. Jesus explained that their relationship with Him would result in pain, hardship, and possibly death. But Jesus also gave them the hope of Heaven.

Additional Questions

- Why did Jesus wait until this time to begin fully unfolding the truth of His death and resurrection?
- Why did Peter refuse to accept the fact that Jesus was going to die?

- Why was Jesus' rebuke to Peter so harshly worded?
- What happens to us spiritually when we try to protect ourselves from pain and hardship?
- What areas of your life are you still "saving" for yourself?
- What things or people do you need to entrust to God's care?
- How does the hope of Heaven motivate you to live for Christ now?

NEXT TIME: Probably the most difficult words to say are "I was wrong." We all hate to admit our weaknesses and failures. As you study the next lesson, you will discover that God wants us to recognize our limitations and weaknesses. When we admit that we need God's help, He can demonstrate His power in us.

LESSON FIVE

A POWERFUL DEMONSTRATION

When Jesus described to the disciples what they could expect in the near future, He also said that some of them would "not taste death before they see the Son of Man coming in his kingdom" (Matthew 16:28). One might wonder what Jesus meant since all of the disciples died before Christ's return. But three of Jesus' disciples, Peter, James, and John, saw firsthand the power and glory of Christ's Kingdom when He was transfigured on the mountain top. In all three Gospel accounts, the story of the transfiguration immediately follows this statement of Christ's, so Jesus may have been referring to their glimpse of His glory.

OBJECTIVE: As a result of this lesson, participants will gain a better understanding of who Jesus is and the role He wants to play in their lives.

Opening Questions

- Have you ever been in the presence of a powerful or famous person? How did you feel?
- When have you seen God's power demonstrated in a spectacular way?

JESUS IS TRANSFIGURED ON THE MOUNTAIN

Matthew 17:1-13, Mark 9:2-13, Luke 9:28-36

Additional Information

Jesus continued to reveal more about Himself to the disciples, singling out three of them to observe His transfiguration. While it is impossible to locate the exact place of the transfiguration, it is known to have taken place in the mountains. Most commentators believe that Moses represented the Jewish Law and that Elijah represented the Prophets. Their appearance on the mount of transfiguration emphasized that the unity of their messages was found in Jesus as the crucified and resurrected Christ.

Additional Questions

- Why had Jesus gone up into the mountains with Peter, James, and John?
- Why do you think He only took these three disciples?
- Why was Jesus transfigured at this particular time in His ministry?
- At what other time did God audibly speak about His Son? (Matthew 3:17, Luke 3:22)
- How do these two events compare?
- What can we learn from this passage about the relationship Jesus has with God the Father?
- How has God revealed Himself to you?

JESUS HEALS A DEMON-POSSESSED BOY

Matthew 17:14-21, Mark 9:14-29, Luke 9:37-43

Additional Information

The day after the transfiguration Jesus and the three disciples rejoined the others who were faced with a problem they couldn't handle. When Jesus heard that the disciples had been unable to heal a demon-possessed boy, He was exasperated and frustrated with their lack of faith. Jesus wanted the disciples to understand how crucial faith and dependence on God would be for their future ministry. Jesus wants all of us to tap into God's unlimited power, instead of relying on our own strength. We can expect only failure if we rely on our own abilities, but we can accomplish great things if we put our faith in God. He delights in demonstrating His power in us.

Additional Questions

- What can you learn about faith from this episode?
- What problems exist in our lives that only Jesus can solve?
- How does unbelief limit God's power?
- When have you had to pray, "Lord, help my unbelief"?
- How did God answer your prayer?

JESUS PREDICTS HIS DEATH THE SECOND TIME

Matthew 17:22-23, Mark 9:30-32, Luke 9:44-45

Additional Information

For the second time Jesus predicted that He would suffer and die, and He also offered the hope of His resurrection. But the disciples only heard the bad news and became discouraged. All their hopes of being part of Christ's glorious kingdom were dashed by Jesus' apparent preoccupation with death. They were so distraught by Jesus' words about His future suffering, that they didn't listen to the good news that His death would be temporary and would bring victory over sin. They didn't realize that Jesus had to die for the sins of the world to establish God's Kingdom.

Additional Questions

- Why do you think the disciples were afraid to ask Jesus to explain His words?
- Can you think of a time when you have been unable, unwilling, or afraid to ask Jesus about something?
- Why did you feel this way?
- How can this passage encourage those who feel discouraged about their ability to understand and apply Scripture?

PETER FINDS THE COIN IN THE FISH'S MOUTH

Matthew 17:24-27

Additional Information

As they returned to Capernaum, Peter was confronted by the tax collector who wanted Jesus' temple tax. Jesus used the situation to teach about Himself. "Jesus, as a Jew, was just as much under obligation to comply with this particular law as with any other. Nor was there any peculiar indignity, either in kind or degree, involved in obeying that law. Doubtless it was a great indignity and humiliation to the Son of God to be paying taxes for the maintenance of His own Father's house!"[8]

Additional Questions

- Why was Jesus so careful not to give offense to the officials regarding this tax, when He had been so confrontational toward the Pharisees earlier?

- Why do you think Jesus used this strange method of raising money for personal needs?
- If you had been in Peter's position, what would you have learned from this experience?

NEXT TIME: The world tries to convince us that we can "have our cake and eat it, too." But in spiritual matters, we can't have it both ways—we must choose whether we will live for ourselves or for God. The first lesson in *Following Jesus* will contrast the world's goals with God's priorities. You will be challenged to follow Jesus' example of serving, instead of seeking the best this world has to offer.

Following Jesus

LESSON ONE

BETTER THAN THE BEST

When Jesus arrived in Jerusalem, He began what has been called the later Judean ministry. He taught in the capital city and in the surrounding province of Judea for a period of about three months, from the Feast of Tabernacles to the Feast of Dedication. Jesus kept His presence in Jerusalem quiet at first, then came out publicly by teaching in the temple area during the middle of the Feast of Tabernacles.

OBJECTIVE: As a result of this lesson, participants will see the difference between the world's goals and God's priorities. They will be challenged to forego seeking the world's best, and instead follow Jesus' perfect example of humble service.

Opening Questions

- What do you view as your greatest accomplishment up to this point in your life?
- If you could be the "world's greatest" in a particular sport or career, what would you choose to be?

JESUS WARNS AGAINST TEMPTATION

Matthew 18:1-35, Mark 9:33-50, Luke 9:46-50

Additional Information

The episode with the temple tax served as an illustration of humility, which led into Jesus' discourse on humility and forgiveness.

Jesus knew the disciples had been arguing over who would be the greatest in His Kingdom. Their pride and desire for status distracted them from what was most important—trusting in God and humbly serving others.

Jesus also gave guidelines for dealing with people who sin against us. Instead of seeking revenge or allowing bitterness to take root in our hearts, Jesus tells us to first go to the person who has wronged us and try to settle our differences privately. Bringing relational problems before the entire church should be a last resort. The religious teachers taught that it was necessary to forgive a person only three times, but Jesus instructs us to forgive others seventy-seven times—as often as is necessary!

Additional Questions

- What need in the disciples' lives caused Jesus to present this discourse at this time (Mark 9:33-37)?
- Why does God value the prayers of children?
- What childlike qualities does Jesus want us to emulate?
- In what practical ways can we "seek the lost"?
- What kinds of difficulties may we face in taking the initiative to confront a brother who has sinned against us?
- What are some things we can do to make sure that our reproof is motivated by love and a desire to restore fellowship instead of a desire to hurt or get even?
- How should we treat a brother who does not want to be forgiven or doesn't admit he has sinned?

JESUS TEACHES ABOUT THE COST OF FOLLOWING HIM

Matthew 8:18-22, 19:1-2; Mark 10:1; Luke 9:51-62; John 7:2-9

Additional Information

> "The visit of Jesus in Galilee after His return from Caesarea Philippi had been brief and of a very private character. All Galilee was now astir in preparation for the annual caravan to the feast which would start in a few days. Jesus had not been in Judea for [some] months. His work of itinerant evangelist in Judea had been cut short at that time because the Jews were seeking to kill Him. . . . He was fully conscious of the near approach of His death, resurrection and ascension on high. He Himself 'set His

face with fixedness of purpose' in spite of all difficulty and danger, 'to go to Jerusalem.'"[1]

Additional Questions

- ▶Why didn't Jesus make an issue of the Samaritans' failure to receive Him (Luke 9:51-56)?
- ▶What excuses do people use today to reject Christ's call?
- ▶Why does Christ expect so much from His followers?
- ▶How can you make sure that you are not resisting Christ's claim to discipleship on your life?

JESUS TEACHES OPENLY AT THE TEMPLE
John 7:10-53

Additional Information

> "[The Feast of Tabernacles] was the holiest and greatest of the feasts of the Jews, intended to commemorate the wanderings of the Israelites through the desert. . . .
>
> "The feast followed on the heels of the great day of Atonement, when sacrifices were made for all the sins of the people. It was celebrated with great joy, the Law being read daily, and seventy bullocks being sacrificed for the seventy nations of the world, in token of Messianic ingathering of the nations."[2]

During the first seven days of the Feast of Tabernacles, the priests would pour water, from the Pool of Siloam, into the silver basin on the west side of the altar of burnt offering.

> "A multitude of pilgrims also marched around the city with music and shouts in commemoration of the taking of Jericho. Others passed the Brook of Siloam to drink, while chanting the words of Isaiah: 'Ho everyone that thirsteth. . . . With joy shall ye draw water from the wells of salvation' (Isaiah 12:3).
>
> "It was near this procession doubtless that Jesus was standing, moved by the enthusiasm of the people, but saddened by the delusion which mistook mere ceremony for religion—the symbol for the reality. Water was a magic word in that sultry dry climate. Raising His voice suddenly

until it sounded out in soft clearness over the throng He cried: 'If anyone thirst let him come to Me and let him drink!' He had the water of life for everyone who would come. The water from Siloam was only a type; He offered them the reality."[3]

Additional Questions

- In what ways do you think the religious leaders intimidated or threatened people?
- What is the sole condition for receiving the Holy Spirit?
- What do your neighbors and coworkers say about Jesus?
- How can believers help one another become more effective witnesses for Christ?
- When have you felt embarrassed or scared to stand up for your faith?
- Who is one person you could begin to tell about your faith in Jesus?

NEXT TIME: People say that "You can't get something for nothing!" But you will learn in the next lesson that the most wonderful gift of all—eternal life—is free. As you study Christ's teaching, you will discover how you can receive this free gift. The next lesson will also expose some misconceptions people have about how to get to Heaven.

LESSON TWO
WITHOUT A DOUBT!

Rather than viewing the Scriptures as guidelines for holy living, the religious leaders were enslaved by the countless rules they had added to the law. Their stubborn adherence to tradition blinded them to the truth that Jesus taught about the Kingdom of Heaven. In fact, they had lost sight of the purpose of the law—their goal was to impress others, not God. The religious leaders had devoted their entire lives to studying and teaching religion, but Jesus revealed that such things do not secure a person's place in Heaven.

OBJECTIVE: As a result of this lesson, participants will understand what they need to do now to enjoy God's presence forever.

Opening Questions

- What do you most look forward to about Heaven?
- What are some misconceptions people have about how to get to Heaven?

JESUS FORGIVES AN ADULTEROUS WOMAN
John 8:1-11

Additional Information

Motivated by their unsuccessful encounters with Jesus and His stinging remarks, such as His statement that tax collectors and harlots would enter the Kingdom of God before them, the religious leaders tried once again to trick Jesus. Bringing a woman caught in adultery before Jesus, they thought He had only two choices—he would either urge them to execute her, which was against Roman law, or He would disobey Old Testament law by setting her free. Either way, they thought they would finally be rid of Him. In their determination to trap Jesus, they had disregarded the law themselves! (When a couple was caught in adultery, the Old Testament required that both the man and woman be stoned. See Leviticus 20:10, Deuteronomy 22:22.)

Additional Questions

- What does this incident reveal about the character of those who brought the woman to Jesus?
- How was the scribes' and Pharisees' question about the adulteress an attempt to trap Jesus?
- How did Jesus' response affect those involved in the incident?
- What did Jesus teach through His answer to the Pharisees' question?
- What are some motives we may have for wanting to see others suffer for their sin?
- Why is it always a dangerous policy to condemn others?

JESUS TEACHES ABOUT HIMSELF

John 8:12-59

Additional Information

The Pharisees thought their strict obedience to the Law would make them acceptable to God. But Jesus told them they would die in their sin unless they believed He was the Son of God. We are *all* helplessly enslaved by sin and no amount of willpower or self-discipline can help us escape its consequences. Jesus is the only person who can free us from the bondage of sin and make us acceptable in God's eyes.

Additional Questions

- What did Jesus mean when He referred to Himself as "I am"?
- In what ways is Jesus the "light of the world"?
- What kind of belief does Jesus ask for in this passage?
- How does sin enslave and control us?
- How does the truth break the power of sin?
- What sin do you need Christ's help to overcome?

JESUS HEALS A BLIND MAN
John 9:1-41

Additional Information
This passage portrays a kind of hardhearted legalism and lack of compassion—typical of the Pharisees. They would have chosen to let a man suffer rather than break even the least of their rules. They fiercely debated Jesus' act of healing a blind man on the Sabbath. According to their long list of regulations, making clay and healing a person were both forbidden on the Sabbath. Some claimed that because Jesus had broken the rules He could not be from God; others wondered how a sinner could perform such miracles. Jesus exposed the spiritual blindness of the religious leaders, explaining that their proud, self-sufficient attitude kept them from accepting the truth. We must be careful to guard against this kind of heartless legalism and open our eyes to our need for Christ.

Additional Questions
- What kind of faith did this man have in Jesus before Jesus told him He was the Son of Man?
- How did the blind man's faith grow after his encounter with Jesus?
- How did the people react to this man's testimony?
- What can we learn from this story about how to increase our faith?

NEXT TIME: Most of us have never personally met a shepherd or had much contact with sheep. But to understand why Scripture describes Jesus as the Good Shepherd, we need to learn more about the role and responsibilities of shepherds in Bible times. The next lesson will reveal the significance of this picture of Christ and help us recognize the ways in which we need to be more like shepherds.

FOLLOWING JESUS

LESSON THREE
TENDER LOVING CARE

This lesson looks at Jesus as the Good Shepherd, a meaningful picture when the Palestinian and Old Testament concepts of a shepherd are taken into consideration. In Palestine, a shepherd would lead the sheep by the sound of his voice, which the flock learned to follow. He called only the sheep that belonged to him and even slept in the sheep pen to protect them from wild animals. Unlike a hired hand, who would run away at the first sight of danger, the shepherd would risk his life to save even one of his animals from harm.

The Psalms describe God as a loving shepherd who cares for the needs of His people (Psalm 23:1), and addresses Him as the "Shepherd of Israel" (Psalm 80:1). God appointed "watchmen" to care for Israel, but because they neglected their responsibility (Isaiah 56:9-12), He promised to send a perfect Shepherd who would lovingly care for the needs of His flock (Ezekiel 34:23).

OBJECTIVE: As a result of this lesson, participants will recognize the many ways Christ cares for them and will be motivated to share His love with others.

Opening Questions

- If you lived in Bible times, do you think you would enjoy being a shepherd? Why, or why not?
- What qualifications or character traits do you think would be important for shepherds to have?

JESUS IS THE GOOD SHEPHERD

John 10:1-21

Additional Information

Unlike a hired hand, who abandons the flock in times of danger, a good shepherd faithfully cares for his sheep. Because of the time the shepherd spends with them, the sheep recognize his voice and follow him. Jesus used this illustration to help us understand how He protects and cares for anyone who believes in Him. We face eternal separation from God because of our sin. But Jesus endured the suffering of the cross to save us. He loved us so much that He willingly sacrificed His life.

Additional Questions

- How does it make you feel to know that Jesus knows His sheep and calls them by name?
- What does this passage reveal about the death of Jesus?
- How does Jesus provide for His followers?

JESUS SENDS OUT SEVENTY-TWO MESSENGERS

Luke 10:1-24

Additional Information

The mission on which Jesus sent the seventy new laborers served as training for future ministry. (Some manuscripts and versions have seventy-two workers.) Though this event is recorded only in Luke's Gospel, Jesus' commissioning of the twelve disciples is described in other passages (Matthew 9:37-38, 10:7-16; Mark 6:7-11; Luke 9:3-5). The theme of their message was to be the same as Christ's: "The kingdom of God is near."

Jesus gave specific instructions to the disciples about how to respond to rejection. He explained that the people who witnessed their miracles and heard the gospel message, but chose to reject the Messiah would be harshly judged. Jesus declared that the city of Sodom—which God had destroyed for its wickedness—would fare better on judgment day than these towns. Jesus condemned the cites of Korazin (north of Capernaum, near the Sea of Galilee) and Bethsaida (on the northeast shore of the Sea of Galilee), explaining that the evil cities of Tyre and Sidon would have surely repented had they seen the same miracles. Even Capernaum, Jesus' home base for ministry in Galilee, rejected Him.

Additional Questions

- What was the mission of the disciples?
- How did Jesus equip them for their task?
- What lessons did Jesus teach the seventy through this experience?
- What applications do you see in this passage for your own life?

JESUS TELLS THE PARABLE OF THE GOOD SAMARITAN

Luke 10:25-37

Additional Information

> "The road from Jerusalem to Jericho descended more than three thousand feet in less than fifteen miles through gorges that were infested with robbers."[4]
>
> "The priest and the Levite feared ceremonial defilement from what might have been a corpse for all they knew. This would have cost them the purchase of ashes of a red heifer for purification, the loss of Temple privileges such as eating from the Temple sacrifices during a week of defilement, the arrangement of burial for the corpse, and the rending of a perfectly good garment as a sign of grief. The priest and the Levite quite clearly saw in the victim a threat of personal loss and inconvenience."[5]

Additional Questions

- What do the lawyer's questions reveal about him?
- Why did Jesus tell this man to keep the Law?
- How does the response of the good Samaritan illustrate loving your neighbor as yourself?
- Who is your neighbor?
- What can you learn from this passage about how to treat your neighbors?

JESUS VISITS MARY AND MARTHA

Luke 10:38-42

Additional Information

The home of Mary and Martha was located in Bethany, a village on the eastern side of the Mount of Olives approximately two miles from Jerusalem. While Mary chose to lounge at Jesus' feet and listen to His teaching, Martha busied herself making preparations for the Lord's stay. Although Jesus didn't criticize Martha for serving Him by doing necessary household work, He also didn't tell Mary to get up and help her sister. Mary's choice to spend time with the Lord was clearly the better choice.

Like Martha, we can become so consumed by the demands of ministry that we lose perspective of what is most important. Jesus desires our worship and adoration. Before we immerse ourselves in ministry, Jesus wants us to sit quietly at His feet and enjoy His presence.

Additional Questions

- How did Jesus evaluate the responses of the two women?
- How can you keep a good balance between listening to Christ and being active in work for Him?
- What conflict have you experienced between service and devotion?
- What first step can you take this week to begin to resolve this conflict?

NEXT TIME: Although Jesus healed the physically blind, His main purpose was to heal the spiritually blind. In the next lesson, we will learn from the example of the religious leaders what can keep us from seeing and accepting spiritual truth. We will be challenged to allow Jesus to remove any blinders from our eyes, so that we can know and obey Him better.

FOLLOWING JESUS

LESSON FOUR

SHARPER VISION

✣

As Jesus traveled the Judean countryside, He taught about discipleship and dealt with false concepts the religious leaders were teaching. The Pharisees continued to challenge Him and tried to expose Him as an impostor.

OBJECTIVE: As a result of this lesson, participants will gain a better understanding of Christ's teaching about Himself and His Kingdom.

Opening Questions

- ▶When has the truth been hard for you to swallow?
- ▶What kinds of things can blind us to the truth about ourselves or our circumstances?

JESUS TEACHES HIS DISCIPLES ABOUT PRAYER

Matthew 6:9-15, Luke 11:1-13

Additional Information

Jesus gave the disciples a pattern for praying, now called the Lord's Prayer. The first line, "Our Father in heaven, hallowed be your name," shows the importance of honoring God's holy name and offering Him our praise and adoration. When Jesus told the disciples to pray "Your kingdom come," they may have secretly hoped this would mean Israel's freedom from political oppression, but Jesus came to establish God's reign in the hearts of believers. "Your will be done on earth as it is in heaven" reveals the desire of believers to see

God's purposes fulfilled instead of their own. When we ask God to "Give us today our daily bread," we are admitting our need for the Lord to provide for us. Jesus also emphasized the importance of asking for God's forgiveness, as well as forgiving others. Finally, the Lord's Prayer encourages believers to ask for God's help to withstand temptation. Jesus' words reveal that we cannot always escape temptation, but God can help us recognize and overcome it.

Additional Questions

- How would you explain the Lord's Prayer to someone who had never heard it before?
- In what ways do you think the order of this prayer is important?
- How can the Lord's Prayer be used as a pattern for personal prayer?
- How does this prayer cut across the desires of human nature?
- Do you think we should repeat this prayer exactly as it is, or should we use it in some other way?
- What reasons are given for persevering in prayer?
- What are some hindrances to prayer?
- How can we overcome them?

JESUS EXPOSES THE RELIGIOUS LEADERS

Luke 11:37–12:12

Additional Information

Similar cures and teachings took place on different occasions in the ministry of Jesus. Partial repetition of the same teachings, as well as similar charges by His enemies, would be answered by substantially the same arguments Jesus had used before. The Pharisees probably brought the same charges many times to disrupt His work in a variety of locations. Once again when Jesus cast a demon out of a dumb man, the crowd marveled and certain leaders accused Him of doing so by the power of the devil (see Matthew 12:24). Other enemies again sought a sign from Heaven under a pretense of piety.

Jesus used the occasion of a dinner at the home of a Pharisee to expose a major sin in the religious community. The act of ceremonial washing had become inordinately important to the Pharisees. This act had lost its purpose, and though everyone else probably practiced it, Jesus noticeably did not.

Additional Questions

- Why was it impossible for Jesus to cast out demons by the power of Beelzebub?

- What was one of the Pharisees' basic misconceptions (Luke 11:38-41)?
- What was the main point of each of the six woes that Jesus pronounced on the religious leaders (11:42-52)?
- What are some of our modern-day practices that would bring forth woes by Jesus?
- What is the relationship between faith and obedience?
- What implications for spiritual leaders today are contained in Jesus' words against the Pharisees?
- By showing us what God hates, what do these words of Jesus tell us about God's nature and what is important to Him?

JESUS WARNS THE PEOPLE

Luke 12:13–13:21

Additional Information

> "The consequence of the bold attack of Jesus on the whole system of Pharisaic and Scribal traditionalism was to precipitate great antagonism on the part of His enemies and draw about Him a vast throng of people [tens of thousands]. Many of them were curiosity-mongers who desired to witness the debate between the discerning Rabbi [Jesus] and the keen lawyers, whose undying enmity He had incurred by His deliberate and daring denunciation of them. In the vast throng, there [probably] were many determined and enraged enemies, a considerable group of disciples, not a few sympathetic friends who had not yet become professed disciples, and many others, who were either indifferent or slightly prejudiced for or against Jesus.
>
> "In the midst of these conditions of a varied assembly, Jesus wisely began His discourse, which would cover many topics according to the needs, by first addressing His disciple-group primarily, but in the presence of the vast multitude, so vast that they trampled on one another to get close enough to hear the speaker."[6]

Additional Questions

- How do the illustrations of the mustard seed and leaven relate to Jesus' warnings (Luke 13:18-21)?

▶Which of these warnings do you feel relate most to the issues and struggles you are dealing with in your own life right now?
▶What can we do to prepare for Christ's return to earth, according to the guidelines He gives us in Luke 12:35-48?

RELIGIOUS LEADERS SURROUND JESUS AT THE TEMPLE
John 10:22-42

Additional Information
The Feast of the Dedication was not biblical in origin. It was begun in 164 B.C. by Judas Maccabeus, a Jewish patriot who led his people to victory over the Syrians, who controlled Palestine at the time. Antiochus Epiphanes, the ruler of Syria from 175 to 164 B.C., hated the Jews and had desecrated the temple some six years earlier. On winning their independence from the Syrians, the Jews celebrated by rededicating and purifying the temple at this feast. "The feast took place in December, toward the end of the month, and would thus be about three months later than the Feast of Tabernacles mentioned in [John] 7:2."[7]

Additional Questions
▶How did Jesus respond to the Jews' accusation?
▶What promises did He make to those who believe?
▶For what reason did the Jews want to stone Jesus?

NEXT TIME: Many Christians are willing to give God ten percent of their income and a couple of hours on Sunday morning, but God wants so much more from us! The next lesson will reveal He wants to be involved in helping us choose our friends. As we look at the kind of people Jesus befriended, we will be challenged to reevaluate our own choices.

FOLLOWING JESUS

LESSON FIVE

A TRUE FRIEND

As Jesus began His last journey to Jerusalem, He was rejected at the Samaritan border (Luke 9:51-53). So He crossed the Jordan River into Perea, a long strip of land on the east bank of the river. (Perea itself is not a New Testament name; it was usually referred to by the Jews as "the land beyond the Jordan" (Matthew 19:1, Mark 3:8). In Perea Jesus entered a new phase of His ministry, teaching and preparing His disciples for the time He would no longer be with them.

OBJECTIVE: As a result of this lesson, participants will see what kind of friend Jesus was and what character traits He valued in others. They will learn from His example how to be a true friend.

Opening Questions

- What do you have in common with your closest friends?
- When have you befriended someone who was very different than you?

JESUS HEALS AND TEACHES PEOPLE

Luke 13:22–14:24

Additional Information

Jesus spoke boldly to His disciples and a great crowd of people, again cutting across the Jewish tradition system. His primary goal before this mixed audience was to address His disciples on the topic of hypocrisy. He had warned them against the corrupt teachings and examples of the Sadducees, Pharisees, and Herodians earlier in His ministry. Now He showed the foolishness of such living.

Pretending concern for Jesus, the Pharisees warned Him of Herod Antipas' intention to kill Him. (Herod Antipas was the son of Herod the Great, who had ordered all male children in Bethlehem murdered. Like his father, he was superstitious, cunning, and totally immoral. After Christ's death, he was stripped of his power by Caesar Caius Caligula and banished to France, where he died in exile.)

Additional Questions

- When asked if few would be saved, what did Jesus bring out in His answer (Luke 13:22-30)?
- How did Jesus answer the warning of the Pharisees (13:31-35)?
- Why was Jesus determined to go to Jerusalem (13:31-35)?
- Why do you think Jerusalem, the center of Jewish religion, was so hardened against Jesus Christ?
- What did Jesus teach about the Sabbath (14:1-6)?
- How is this teaching about the Sabbath relevant today?
- What lesson can we learn from the parable of the great feast about witnessing or trying to lead someone into a life of discipleship?
- Why do so many people refuse spiritual riches and instead seek earthly wealth?

JESUS TEACHES ABOUT THE COST OF BEING A DISCIPLE

Luke 14:25-35

Additional Information

With large crowds trailing behind Him, Jesus traveled toward Jerusalem and His impending death. Wanting the crowds to think through their enthusiasm for Him, Jesus began to explain the cost of following Him. He announced to the crowd that anyone who wanted to be His disciple had to "hate" his parents, siblings, even his own life. (In this passage, the term translated as *hate* expresses choosing one over another or prizing one more dearly.) Jesus warned them that anyone who would not "carry his cross" to follow Him could not be His disciple. The Jews knew full well that carrying a cross showed a person's complete submission—the Romans forced criminals to carry the crosses upon which they would be crucified. Jesus' shocking words were meant to challenge the people to evaluate the depth of their commitment.

Additional Questions

- What is the price to be paid for discipleship?
- What does it mean to count the cost of being a disciple?
- In what ways does Jesus want us to be like salt?
- Under what condition can we blame circumstances, people, or other reasons for our not following Christ?
- How should feelings of weakness and incompetence affect our discipleship?
- What changes do you need to make in your personal life to better represent Christ to the world around you?

JESUS TELLS THREE PARABLES

Luke 15:1-32

Additional Information

Once again Jesus spoke to His disciples in parables. The first parable in this series had to do with a lost sheep. The people of Perea raised many sheep and were familiar with the ways of shepherds. If the owner of a herd, who may have been the shepherd, missed even one sheep, he would seek it till he found it; he would then carry it back to the flock in his arms.

The second parable was also about losing, searching, and finding. The poor woman lost a small silver coin in her dark and windowless hut. It was probably a tenth of a cherished dowry handed down by her family. Her coin may have borne the image of a Roman emperor, but man bears the image of God and is of infinitely greater value.

The lost son parable shows the grace of God—first from the divine side, then from the human side. In the prodigal son we see the development of an attitude that leads to repentance. As the younger son, he would have received one-third of the estate, his older brother two-thirds. In that culture, early dividing of the estate carried with it the responsibility by law to care for the father, a principle which the younger brother seemed to ignore. After he had wasted his inheritance, he had to resort to feeding swine for a Gentile, a practice abhorrent to the Jews. Finally, reason got the upper hand over sensual appetite, and he returned to his father in repentance and humility.

Additional Questions

- What stimulated Jesus to give these parables?
- What is taught in these three parables about values, being lost, searching, and finding?

- How are the Pharisees' attitudes brought out in each of these parables?
- What can we do if we find that we are unconcerned about people who are lost?
- How do these parables relate to our presentation of the gospel?
- In light of these parables, what changes do you need to make in your attitude toward evangelism and missions?

NEXT TIME: The way we manage money reveals a lot more about ourselves than we might think. In the first lesson of book five, you will study Jesus' radical teaching about money. You will be challenged to consider what your checkbook would look like if you truly lived by Kingdom values.

Answering the Call

LESSON ONE
A RADICAL APPROACH

Scholars differ on the chronology of this period of Jesus' ministry. If He raised Lazarus from the dead at the time presented in this Bible study, Jesus may have traveled to Ephraim after that notable miracle (John 11:54), and from there returned to Perea. He then may have come to Jerusalem through Jericho (Luke 19:1,28). Others suggest Jesus stopped in Jericho on His way to Bethany, where after raising Lazarus He went to Ephraim for a short stay, then returned to Bethany and on to Jerusalem.

OBJECTIVE: As a result of this lesson, participants will better understand Jesus' teaching on how to live by Kingdom values, particularly in financial matters. They will be challenged to adjust their habits and lifestyle to correspond with Jesus' radical teaching about stewardship.

Opening Questions

- Why do you think so many people are preoccupied with accumulating and managing money?
- How can you tell if a person loves money?
- As you have matured as a believer, how has your view of money changed?

JESUS TEACHES HIS DISCIPLES
Luke 16:1–17:10

Additional Information
Jesus continued His ministry by teaching about faith and stewardship. He directed a parable to His disciples, then told a story to the Pharisees, and finally another parable to the disciples. We learn from this passage that our use of money reveals our faith in God. As believers, we must use our money and resources in a way that increases our faith and honors God, the source of all wealth.

Additional Questions
- What does the parable of the rich man and Lazarus teach about money and life after death?
- In what ways would obeying Jesus' teaching in this passage change the average person's lifestyle today?
- What is our true responsibility to people who are destitute, as Lazarus was?
- How was the parable an answer to the disciples' request to increase their faith (Luke 17:7-10)?

JESUS RAISES LAZARUS FROM THE DEAD
John 11:1-44

Additional Information
When Jesus heard that His friend Lazarus was severely ill, He was teaching His disciples in Bethabara (sometimes called Bethany beyond the Jordan). This Lazarus was a well-to-do friend of Jesus, the brother of Mary and Martha, and should not be confused with Lazarus the beggar of the story in the preceding section (Luke 16:19-31).

Imagine the frustration and distress Mary and Martha felt as their brother died of his illness while Jesus tarried in Perea. Their days of anxiety—not knowing why Jesus had not come—no doubt prepared them for the important lessons He would teach them.

Additional Questions
- What is revealed about the disciples in their response to Jesus' suggestion that they go to Judea?
- What can we learn from this passage about the purpose of suffering?

- When have you seen God's power demonstrated in an amazing way?
- How has your faith been affected by answered prayer?
- How have you been affected by unanswered prayer?

JESUS HEALS TEN MEN WITH LEPROSY
Luke 17:11-19

Additional Information

As He traveled south to Jerusalem, along the border between Samaria and Galilee, Jesus encountered ten men with leprosy. This disease was characterized by nodules under the skin which enlarged and spread. There was loss of sensation and eventual paralysis, wasting of muscle, and resultant deformities and mutilations. All lepers were treated as social outcasts. The Gospel writer also identifies one of the men as a Samaritan—a race the Jews detested. Normally Jews would go out of their way to avoid these men, but Jesus demonstrated that He had come to minister to all kinds of people by healing them. Only one of the ten, the Samaritan, returned to thank Jesus. Jesus' response to him—"Your faith has made you well"—reveals that he may have also received spiritual healing.

Additional Questions

- What is significant about the one healed leper who returned?
- If you had been one of the nine, what might some of your excuses be for not returning to Jesus?
- How can you avoid making such excuses today?
- What is the most important lesson you have learned from this incident?

NEXT TIME: We've learned in previous lessons that we have to sacrifice certain things to enter God's Kingdom. The next lesson will reveal the benefits of being included in the Kingdom of God. You will also discover how the Holy Spirit can help you stand strong until Christ returns.

LESSON TWO
IN OUR HEARTS

The crowds, the religious leaders, even Jesus' own disciples, had wrong ideas and expectations about the Kingdom of God. Jesus continued to expose these misconceptions—He explained that entrance into His Kingdom was by God's grace alone. By reaching out to the lowest members of society, Jesus demonstrated that God welcomes *all* people into His Kingdom.

OBJECTIVE: As a result of this lesson, participants will gain a better understanding of what it means to be included in God's Kingdom and the difference His Spirit can make in their lives.

Opening Questions

- When you were a child, what do you remember being taught about Heaven?
- How do you think your life would be different if you didn't believe in Heaven?

JESUS TEACHES ABOUT THE KINGDOM OF GOD
Luke 17:20-37

Additional Information
Once again Jesus predicted His suffering and death, explaining that it was a necessary step in God's plan for the world. Jesus also spoke of His imminent return, but warned His followers to watch out for people who claim they know when it will happen. Instead of trying

to predict the exact time, Jesus wants us to be ready every day for His return. Scripture tells us all we need to know—His return will be sudden and evident to all the world. Until then, Christ wants us to continue living for Him. Our future hope of Heaven should motivate us to live according to different priorities than people who think this life is all there is.

Additional Questions

- What misconceptions did the Pharisees have about who God is and what He is like?
- What can we learn about the Second Coming from the climactic events of Noah's and Lot's times?
- Why were the times of Noah and Lot picked as examples?
- How do the conditions during Noah's and Lot's times parallel conditions in our own time?
- What significance is there in that both Noah and Lot escaped the judgments of their day? Why did they escape?
- How can we prepare for Christ's Second Coming?

JESUS TELLS TWO PARABLES ON PRAYER

Luke 18:1-14

Additional Information

The first parable in this passage describes a widow who eventually received justice from an uncaring judge because of her persistence. Because she had no family to stick up for her, she was especially vulnerable and helpless. All she could do was pester the judge until he was compelled to help her. This parable reveals the importance of always bringing our needs before the Lord in prayer. Our prayers may not be answered immediately, but we can always be sure that He hears us and knows what is best for us.

The second parable shows the difference between praying to gain recognition from others and praying out of a desire to know God better. The Pharisee announced his good works to all within earshot, but the tax collector privately admitted his sin and begged for God's mercy. Jesus explained that pride cuts us off from God, but humility pleases Him.

Additional Questions

- To whom did Jesus tell these parables?
- Why does God delay answers to prayer?

- How should we approach God when we pray?
- How can you develop a spirit of humility in your prayer life?

JESUS TEACHES ABOUT MARRIAGE AND DIVORCE
Matthew 19:3-12, Mark 10:2-12

Additional Information

As Jesus was on His way to Jerusalem, the Pharisees once again attempted to trap Him. This particular question dealt with the issue of divorce. Jesus' answers could have brought Him in direct conflict with Herod Antipas, who lived in open adultery with Herodias (she had divorced Herod's brother) and who had imprisoned and murdered John the Baptist over this very issue.

The Hillel school of thought believed it was lawful for a man to get a divorce "for every cause," even for the most trivial offenses. Although Jewish women could not divorce their husbands like Greek and Roman women could, all Jewish men could divorce their wives for such reasons as, finding no favor in his eyes, being thought of as less attractive than another woman, having her head uncovered in public, speaking to another man, burning her husband's bread, or being childless for ten years. This school, naturally, was the more popular in Palestine and its teachings led to a general moral laxity among the people. The Shammai school, on the other hand, allowed few causes for a man to divorce his wife. So if Jesus took this position, many would be offended.

Additional Questions

- Why is there so much confusion among Christians today about divorce and remarriage?
- In His remarks about divorce, what does Jesus indicate is the primary fact to consider?
- What is God's purpose in a man and a woman joining together in marriage?
- What steps can you take now to become a better spouse in the future?

JESUS BLESSES LITTLE CHILDREN

Matthew 19:13-15, Mark 10:13-16, Luke 18:15-17

Additional Information

Jesus loved children! When His followers brought their little ones to Him, Jesus laid His hands on them, blessing them and praying for them. He rebuked the disciples for turning them away, explaining that children show us the kind of faith we need to enter the Kingdom of God. Jesus' actions also reveal that God's grace is given freely to those who humbly accept it.

Additional Questions

- How do you typically find yourself treating children?
- In what ways do you think your church needs to place a higher importance on children's ministries?
- In what ways could you value and care for the children in your church?
- What is one childlike attribute you would like to cultivate this next week?

NEXT TIME: Have you ever wished there were more hours in a day? So many different things demand our attention—work obligations, family responsibilities, and needs in the church and community—that we often feel overwhelmed by it all. The next lesson will encourage you to evaluate your priorities. You'll discover that if you give God first place in your life, He will guide you in all other areas of life.

LESSON THREE
FIRST PLACE

✣

The importance of Jesus' last week before the cross may be seen in the space given to it by the Gospel writers. Matthew and Mark devote about a third of their books to the events of Passion Week and Jesus' resurrection. A little less than a quarter of Luke's Gospel and nearly half of John's Gospel record this same period. This emphasis is appropriate, since Jesus' death and resurrection are the major purpose for His coming into our world. He triumphantly embarked on the last stage of His mission.

OBJECTIVE: As a result of this lesson, participants will be challenged to identify what interferes with their obedience to God. They will also be reminded of the rewards Jesus promises to those who sacrifice their own desires to follow Him.

Opening Questions

- What would you say is your most valued possession?
- On a scale of 1 to 10, how difficult do you think it would be for you to sell your car(s) and rely on public transportation?

JESUS SPEAKS TO THE RICH YOUNG MAN

Matthew 19:16–20:16, Mark 10:17-31, Luke 18:18-30

Additional Information

That a rich young ruler would seek Jesus out must have seemed incredible to many who witnessed this incident. The man was probably a member of an official council, yet approached Jesus for spiritual advice. Unfortunately, the man's wealth kept him from following Jesus' instructions. Jesus followed this conversation with a discussion with His disciples and a parable on the Kingdom of Heaven.

Additional Questions

- If the young ruler had indeed kept the whole law, why do you think he was still unsure of eternal life?
- Why did Jesus tell this man to go and sell all he had, when He had told others that all they had to do was believe?
- Why did Jesus give the illustration of a camel and needle?
- What observation can you make from these incidents regarding your own service for Jesus Christ?
- How do people today try to find security and fulfillment?
- What place should money have in your life?

JESUS TEACHES ABOUT SERVING OTHERS

Matthew 20:17-28, Mark 10:32-45, Luke 18:31-34

Additional Information

Tradition suggests that Salome was the mother of James and John (Mark 15:40). She is also considered to be Mary's sister (John 19:25), making the two men Jesus' cousins. Her request makes it obvious that she did not correctly understand the Kingdom of God.

Additional Questions

- What did Jesus tell His disciples about His impending death and resurrection?
- Why were Jesus' followers amazed and afraid?
- What had taken place shortly before the mother's request for her sons?
- Why did Jesus answer her as He did?
- What important lesson did Jesus teach His disciples about service?

JESUS HEALS A BLIND BEGGAR

Matthew 20:29-34, Mark 10:46-52, Luke 18:35-43

Additional Information

Jericho was situated on the same site as the city Joshua captured nearly 1,450 years earlier. But it was not the same city, since Joshua had totally destroyed that ancient Jericho and had pronounced a curse against anyone who might rebuild it (Joshua 6:21-26). Nonetheless, Jericho was rebuilt in the days of King Ahab by Hiel, on whom Joshua's curse was literally fulfilled (1 Kings 16:34).

> "Matthew mentions two blind men, while Mark and Luke describe one, probably the more conspicuous one. The discrepancy as to place, 'as He went out from Jericho,' 'as He drew nigh unto Jericho,' is best explained by the recent suggestion that the healing occurred after He left the old Jericho, and as He was approaching the new Jericho which Herod the Great had built at some distance away."[1]

Additional Questions

▶What was there in this beggar that attracted Jesus to him?
▶How did the blind man respond to the crowd's rebuke?
▶What did the blind man ask of Jesus?
▶For what specific reason did Jesus offer the man healing?
▶How did the blind man express his gratitude to Jesus?
▶What can you learn from Bartimaeus's example?

NEXT TIME: "Long live the King!" The next lesson looks at Jesus' triumphal entry into Jerusalem and how the people reacted. As you study the events leading up to and including Jesus' arrival in Jerusalem, you will gain a better understanding of Christ's lordship.

ANSWERING THE CALL

LESSON FOUR
WHILE YOU WAIT

✣

Jesus told His disciples that He was going to prepare a place for His followers. This new heaven and new earth (Isaiah 65:17, 66:22; Revelation 21:1) will be far better than we can ever imagine. Our greatest joy will be living in God's presence forever. While we can be confident that the best is yet to come, God wants us to serve and obey Him while we await this glorious future. The knowledge that we will spend eternity with God should give us the courage to endure the trials and temptations of this life.

OBJECTIVE: As a result of this lesson, participants will learn that although the Kingdom of God will not be fully established on earth until Jesus returns, He wants to be the King of their lives now.

Opening Questions

- What red-letter day do you most look forward to?
- Does not knowing the exact details of a future event usually increase or decrease the joy of anticipation? Explain.

JESUS BRINGS SALVATION TO ZACCHAEUS'S HOME

Luke 19:1-10

Additional Information

"The city of Jericho was an important center for the collection of internal revenue. The head of the civil service department held a position of great influence in the political structure of that time. The method of collecting taxes was open to wide abuse, which made the populace regard those in the profession with hatred and contempt. The Jews were among the most heavily taxed people of the ancient world, and it is not difficult to imagine their resentment toward anyone connected with the system. Some collectors were notorious for extortion. Among these was Zacchaeus, one of the chief tax officers in Jericho. He may have been the most unpopular man in the whole city."[2]

Additional Questions

- How did everyone else respond to Jesus' decision to befriend Zacchaeus?
- How did Zacchaeus react to Jesus' interest in him?
- What do Zacchaeus's words and actions indicate about his changed attitude?
- How does a person's reputation usually affect the way we treat him or her? Why?
- What do Jesus' actions teach us about how to treat the less desirable people in our communities?
- In what ways can we reach out to people with less than perfect reputations?

JESUS TELLS THE PARABLE OF THE KING'S TEN SERVANTS
Luke 19:11-27

Additional Information

The parable of the pounds (KJV) or *minas* (NIV) in Luke is different in many details from that of the talents (Matthew 25:14-30) and serves a different purpose. Here a nobleman goes to obtain a kingdom and makes his servants responsible for a certain amount of money to see how they manage it. "The pound was worth about $20, which was about three months' wages at the time."[3]

Additional Questions

- What is the difference between a talent and a *mina*? (The reference helps at the back of your Bible may contain a table of weights and measures that explains this.)
- What is meant by the statement about taking away minas from the poor and giving them to the rich?

▶How does this parable relate to Jesus?
▶When have you seen some practical examples of this principle (Luke 19:26)?
▶How are these parables significant and applicable to you?
▶How do we use what God has given us for our own advancement or benefit?

RELIGIOUS LEADERS PLOT TO KILL JESUS

John 11:45-57, 12:9-11

Additional Information

Jesus arrived in Bethany, fifteen miles from Jericho, in the month Nisan (March/April), six days before the Passover celebration. This feast lasted a week, but the Passover supper would be held on Thursday evening. Thousands of pilgrims poured into Jerusalem at this time, set up their tents, and purified themselves in preparation for this all-important feast.

Lazarus had been raised from the dead about six weeks before. When Jesus' whereabouts were known, many common people flocked to see both Him and Lazarus, but the religious leaders wanted to arrest Him.

Additional Questions

▶What kind of thoughts do you think were running through the minds of the religious leaders at this time?
▶Why would Jesus' enemies go after Him at this particular time?

JESUS RIDES INTO JERUSALEM ON A DONKEY

Matthew 21:1-11,14-17; Mark 11:1-11; Luke 19:28-44; John 12:12-13

Additional Information

The palm was the symbol of beauty and of the righteous man (Psalm 92:12-14). A palm branch was used to signify the "head," the highest of the people, and was associated with rejoicing as well as with triumph and victory.

Jesus had sent two disciples to a nearby village (probably Bethpage), where a donkey's colt was tied. He had assured them that permission would be given to use the colt (Mark 11:3).

Additional Questions

- What relationship does the raising of Lazarus have to the crowd's enthusiastic reception of Jesus as Messiah?
- What is the significance of Jesus' riding on a colt (Zechariah 9:9)?
- How familiar do you think the disciples would have been with this prophecy?
- What is the significance of the palms and garments spread in Jesus' path?
- What problem did Jesus' actions and the crowd's reaction pose for the Jewish authorities?
- What were their options at this time?
- Why did Jesus weep over Jerusalem?

NEXT TIME: In the next lesson, you'll be surprised to learn that getting angry is sometimes the *right* thing to do! As you look at Jesus' righteous anger over the corrupt religious practices in His Father's house, you will be challenged to evaluate your own attitudes and actions in church.

LESSON FIVE
HE DESERVES IT

The Gospels of Matthew, Mark, and Luke give more space to details on the teachings of Jesus on this one day—in the temple and on the Mount of Olives—than any other.

OBJECTIVE: As a result of this lesson, participants will see how Jesus reacted when He saw activities at the temple interfering with worship. His actions will challenge them to reexamine their own attitudes and actions in God's house.

Opening Questions

- What attracted you to the church you currently attend?
- What common attitudes and activities in the church do you think turn people off to Christianity?

JESUS CURSES THE FIG TREE
Matthew 21:18-19, Mark 11:12-14

Additional Information

Using an object lesson, Jesus communicated an important truth to His disciples. The barren fig tree represented the empty faith of many Jews who participated in the temple activities without ever worshiping God. Our "busyness" in God's house can be as deceiving as the fig tree that was full of leaves but lacked fruit. Our service means nothing unless our focus is on God.

Additional Questions

- How will the Father "honor" those who serve Christ?
- What is the relationship between serving Christ and being with Christ?
- How can we know if our service is pleasing to God?
- How can we find the right balance between worship and service?
- In what ways can we show respect for God's house?
- What steps can you take to make sure your involvement in ministry doesn't interfere with your worship?

JESUS CLEARS THE TEMPLE AGAIN

Matthew 21:12-13, Mark 11:15-19, Luke 19:45-48

Additional Information

In the first cleansing of the temple, Jesus initiated His public ministry and portrayed Himself as a reformer. He boldly condemned the corrupt practices in the temple that distracted people from the true purpose of God's house. Now, three years later, Jesus discovered that the "bazaar of Annas" had been restored. The same greedy merchants had set up their stalls in the court of Gentiles under the pretense of providing their services for foreign travelers who came to Jerusalem to celebrate Passover. In reality, they took advantage of the situation to pad their pockets. The Gentiles from out of town had to change their currency to give the temple tax and to buy animals to sacrifice, so the moneychangers inflated their exchange rates and the merchants raised the prices of the sacrificial animals. Once again Jesus removed the bleating sheep, the sellers of pigeons, and the crying moneychangers. This final demonstration of judgment on the temple system enraged the religious authorities.

Additional Questions

- How are the first and second cleansings of the temple different (see John 2:13-22)?
- Why do you think Jesus was so infuriated by the temple activities?
- Why did Jesus' actions upset the religious leaders?
- Which of the programs or activities at your church do you think distract from worship?

JESUS SUMMARIZES HIS PURPOSE AND MESSAGE
John 12:20-50

Additional Information

Interested in what was happening around them in Jerusalem—the triumphal entry and the cleansing of the temple—some Greeks (probably converts to Judaism) came to see Jesus. Their questions led to another discourse in which Jesus revealed what His death and resurrection would accomplish for the human race. While talking about His impending death, Jesus began to pray to the Father. As a human being, Jesus dreaded the painful death He knew He would have to endure. As the Son of God, He accepted the role God chose for Him in bringing salvation to the world. Although Jesus could have escaped the suffering of the cross, He loved us enough to go through with it.

Additional Questions

- What do Jesus' statements of commitment in John 12:23-26 mean in a practical way?
- What does Jesus teach about His forthcoming death (John 12:23-36)?
- How is the rejection of Jesus explained in John's Gospel (John 12:37-43)?

JESUS SAYS HIS DISCIPLES CAN PRAY FOR ANYTHING
Matthew 21:20-22, Mark 11:20-25

Additional Information

Jesus says that if we have faith we can move mountains! But this isn't a license to pray for miraculous and wondrous signs just for the thrill of it. Jesus was stressing the importance of believing that God can answer our prayers. While faith is an essential ingredient in prayer, we also need to keep in mind the character of God. He will only answer requests that are in line with the principles of His Kingdom, not those that are motivated by selfish desires. Christ gives us a perfect example of how to pray according to God's will.

Additional Questions

- Why is forgiveness connected here to prayer?
- What happens when we hold grudges?

▶What kind of personal application can you draw from Jesus' advice in this passage (Mark 11:25)?

NEXT TIME: Many Bible characters are known for their courage, loyalty, and faith, but there's also a group of people famous for their hypocrisy and greed. The first lesson in *Final Teachings* looks at the mistakes and failures of the Jewish leaders in Jesus' day. As you study their actions and attitudes, you will discover what Jesus wants you to avoid.

Final Teachings

LESSON ONE

LIVE AND LEARN

Early in Jesus' ministry in Galilee, the religious leaders began plotting to destroy Him. By this point, they were more determined and organized in their plan. The different beliefs of the various groups of religious and social leaders usually set them against each other, but they came together to figure out a way to get rid of Jesus.

The Pharisees, who were very influential in the synagogues, separated themselves from anyone who didn't obey both Old Testament Law and the oral traditions of the Jewish rabbis. They believed that God's grace was available only to those who obeyed the Law. Herodians were influential Jews who supported Rome and feared that Jesus would upset the stable political situation. The Sadducees were wealthy upper-class Jews who were primarily concerned with the administration of the temple. They rejected the oral tradition that had been handed down from generation to generation, believing that only the Pentateuch, the five books of Moses, were valid. But these different groups agreed on one point—Jesus was a threat to their religious authority and political stability.

OBJECTIVE: In this lesson, participants will study the example set by the religious leaders in Jesus' day. As they look at their actions and attitudes, they will discover what Jesus wants them to avoid.

Opening Questions

- In what ways are you different from your parents? How are you similar?
- As best as you can remember, how did you feel the first time you realized your parents had made a mistake?

- Why do you think we often make the same mistakes our parents did, even when we can see the consequences of their mistakes?

RELIGIOUS LEADERS CHALLENGE JESUS' AUTHORITY
Matthew 21:23-27, Mark 11:27-33, Luke 20:1-8

Additional Information

The second cleansing of the temple brought Jesus into conflict with the religious leaders once again. Calling Him to account for His actions, they asked Jesus who gave Him the authority to perform an official act like clearing the temple court. This was a common ploy of the religious leaders—they had questioned both John the Baptist (John 1:19-25) and Jesus earlier in His ministry (John 2:18-22). The Jewish leaders were particularly concerned about Jesus' cleansing of the temple because His actions affected their income. They hoped the crowds would begin to distrust Jesus and turn back to them for spiritual leadership.

Additional Questions

- How were the religious leaders' questions designed to trap Jesus?
- How did Jesus' question in turn trap them?
- Why did Jesus refuse to answer after they pleaded ignorance?
- Why do we sometimes feel threatened when people question or confront us about our religious practices?
- Under what circumstances do you find it difficult to submit to God's Word?

JESUS TELLS THREE PARABLES
Matthew 21:28–22:14, Mark 12:1-12, Luke 20:9-19

Additional Information

The hardened hearts of these religious leaders led Jesus to give them three warnings in the form of parables. In the parable of the two sons, Jesus condemned the chief priests and elders for their unbelief, exclaiming that tax collectors and prostitutes would enter the Kingdom of God ahead of them because these sinners had repented and accepted the truth!

In the second parable, Jesus revealed that He knew of their plan to kill Him. In the parable, the landowner is God and the vineyard is the nation of Israel. The tenants represent the Jewish leaders; the servants symbolize the Old Testament prophets and the son is Jesus. The other tenants represent non-Jews who accepted the gospel after many Jews had rejected it.

The parable of the wedding feast depicts God's rejection of Israel and the responsibility of individuals to respond to the gospel message. The wedding garment symbolizes the righteousness of God that He offers to all people. The parable teaches that a person must choose to accept God's invitation in order to enter His banquet—that is, eternal life. (For other Scripture passages that use similar imagery, see Psalm 132:16; Isaiah 61:10; and Revelation 3:4-6, 19:7-9.)

Additional Questions

- Why was Jesus so openly hostile to the religious leaders?
- What do you imagine the crowd thought?
- For what reasons do we sometimes misinterpret or ignore the truth of God's Word?
- In what area of your life have you been resisting God's Word?
- What step of obedience can you take today to more fully submit yourself to God?

RELIGIOUS LEADERS ASK JESUS THREE QUESTIONS

Matthew 22:15-40, Mark 12:13-34, Luke 20:20-40

Additional Information

The Pharisees understood the parables were directed at them and became outraged. Yet they dared not touch Jesus because they feared the people, who now enthusiastically supported Him. The common cause of the three groups—Pharisees, Sadducees, and scribes—led them to ask questions in order to snare Jesus. But Jesus used their trick questions as an opportunity to teach the crowds about His priorities.

Additional Questions

- How did Jesus answer the Pharisees' question about paying taxes?
- How is His answer relevant to us today?
- Why did the Sadducees think that their question about the wife in the resurrection posed an unsolvable problem for Jesus?
- How can you know if you truly love the Lord as Jesus describes (Matthew 22:37)?
- How can you love your neighbors in the sense that Jesus was talking about?

▸How can we guard against misinterpreting the Bible?
▸What current issues or debates distract us from the central truth of the gospel?

RELIGIOUS LEADERS CANNOT ANSWER JESUS' QUESTION

Matthew 22:41-46, Mark 12:35-37, Luke 20:41-44

Additional Information

The religious leaders knew that the Messiah would be the Son of David, but they did not realize that he would also be the Son of God. The verse in Psalm 110 that Jesus referred to is used in Acts 2:34-36 and Hebrews 1:13 to prove Christ's deity. Jesus wanted the Jews to understand that He was both the Messiah and God's Son.

Additional Questions

▸How does the scriptural statement that David's son is also David's Lord relate to this discussion?
▸Why did no one answer Jesus' question?

NEXT TIME: If you think Jesus was the mild-mannered, peace-keeping type, go on to lesson two! Nothing infuriated Jesus more than the hypocrisy of the Pharisees and teachers of the law, and He told them so. As you study His words to them, you'll discover the importance of practicing what you preach.

FINAL TEACHINGS

LESSON TWO
PRACTICE WHAT YOU PREACH!

All the quibbling from the religious leaders had led Jesus to renounce their actions but never their authority. What concerned Him was not what they had to say, but how they applied what they taught. While many of them found ways to get around the laws themselves, they did not lighten the load of the people.

OBJECTIVE: In this lesson, participants will learn from the example of the religious leaders the importance of practicing what they preach. Jesus' harsh criticism of the Jewish leaders will motivate them to examine their own intentions and actions.

Opening Questions

- ▶When you were growing up, who did you admire as a spiritual leader or religious teacher?
- ▶How do our expectations of people change as we grow older?
- ▶How does it feel when people we respect and admire let us down?

JESUS WARNS AGAINST THE RELIGIOUS LEADERS
Matthew 23:1-12, Mark 12:38-40, Luke 20:45-47

Additional Information

It's helpful to note that "Phylacteries were little boxes, attached to the forehead or left arm, containing small strips of parchment with certain Scripture verses written on them. The larger the box, the greater the piety professed by the wearer."[1]

Additional Questions

- ▶What charges of hypocrisy did Jesus levy against the scribes and Pharisees?
- ▶What are some of the ways we can be guilty of doing works only to be seen by others?
- ▶How can we humble ourselves instead?

JESUS CONDEMNS THE RELIGIOUS LEADERS

Matthew 23:13-39

Additional Information

Jesus turned from warning His disciples and the listening people to a direct denunciation of the scribes and Pharisees. The eight woes (seven if verse 14 is excluded as in some versions) were pronounced against the religious leaders because of the outward show they made of knowing God, His prophets, and His laws. Jesus also condemned them for the way their hypocrisy led the common people astray.

Additional Questions

- ▶How did Jesus expose the twisted priorities of the religious leaders?
- ▶What distortion of values does Jesus deal with in these words of denunciation?
- ▶How did the Pharisees overlook justice, mercy, and faithfulness?
- ▶What overall principle was Jesus teaching in this passage?
- ▶What parallels, if any, do you see between the condition and practice of the Pharisees and any current situations among God's people today?

A POOR WIDOW GIVES ALL SHE HAS

Mark 12:41-44, Luke 21:1-4

Additional Information

In this story, Jesus was watching the collection boxes in the court of the women at the temple. There were different boxes in the temple court where people could give their money to the temple treasury. Six boxes were designated for freewill offerings and seven others were for the temple tax that Jewish males were required to give. When Jesus saw the poor widow give all of her money as a freewill offering to God's house, He praised her sacrificial gift, knowing that she had given out of a heart of gratitude.

Additional Questions

- Do you think it was wise for this woman to give everything she had to the church? Why, or why not?
- Do you think God leads people to do this kind of giving today?
- What principles of giving from this passage do you need to apply to your life?
- What does this story reveal about true discipleship?

JESUS TELLS ABOUT THE FUTURE

Matthew 24:1-51, Mark 13:1-37, Luke 21:5-38

Additional Information

As Jesus was leaving the temple, one of His disciples remarked about the grandeur of the buildings. Jesus replied by predicting the destruction of the temple and of Jerusalem, and warning His hearers to flee for their lives when the time of that destruction finally arrived. Scholars tell us, "History indeed records that the faithful in Jerusalem and its environs obeyed the warning of the Savior. When the first signs appeared that Jerusalem was going to be surrounded by the Roman forces (A.D. 70) practically all the Christians fled from the city and its environs across the Jordan to the Trans-Jordanian town of Pella."[2] Later, Jesus sat down on the Mount of Olives, which overlooked Jerusalem and the temple complex, and continued His predictions.

Additional Questions

- What questions did the disciples ask Jesus?
- What is the lesson of the thief in the night (Matthew 24:43-44)?
- What can we know for sure about the return of Christ?
- How should we act if we truly expect Jesus to come back for us?
- What were the differences in attitude between the faithful servant and the wicked servant?

NEXT TIME: The next lesson looks at the life of a traitor. Probably the most despised person in all of Scripture is Judas Iscariot, the man who betrayed Jesus Christ. As you look at his actions, you may be shocked to discover that we are capable of failing the Lord in similar ways. You will also learn what kind of friendship Jesus desires from us.

FINAL TEACHINGS

LESSON THREE
A FAITHFUL FRIEND

In this lesson, Jesus reveals the consequences of rejecting Him. Everyone who refuses to repent will go to a place of eternal punishment when they die. There are several different terms used in Scripture to refer to the place people go after death. The Old Testament used the word Sheol, which means "the grave" to describe the place of the dead (Job 24:19, Psalm 16:10, Isaiah 38:10.) The word used in the New Testament for Sheol is the Greek word Hades (Matthew 16:18; Revelation 1:18, 20:9-10.) The place of eternal fire where God will send Satan, his demons, and all unbelievers is Gehenna—that is, hell (Mark 9:43, James 3:6, Revelation 19:20.) This is where the wicked will spend eternity after the last judgment.

OBJECTIVE: As a result of this lesson, participants will learn what kind of friendship Jesus desires from us.

Opening Questions

- How does it feel to receive an expensive gift from a friend?
- What motivates people to sacrifice their own needs for their friends?
- When has a friend supported and helped you through a difficult time?

JESUS TELLS ABOUT THE FINAL JUDGMENT

Matthew 25:1-46

Additional Information

Through these parables, Jesus emphasizes the importance of being ready at any time for Him because the day and hour of His return are unknown. Until that day when Jesus comes back to gather believers, He wants us to use our God-given gifts and abilities for His glory, not our own. Everyone who believes in Jesus will go to Heaven, but those who have lived selfishly will not receive the same rewards as those who have faithfully served God.

The parable of the sheep and the goats depicts how God will separate believers from unbelievers. While some may think that their good deeds can gain them eternal life, Jesus taught that only those who believe in Christ and reach out to the needy in His name will be rewarded in Heaven. Anyone who rejects Jesus or merely pretends to believe will suffer eternal punishment.

Additional Questions

- In the parable of the ten virgins, why was it necessary to have oil in the lamp?
- What might this oil represent?
- What is the significance of the fact that the bridegroom was delayed?
- What is the relationship between "talents" and spiritual gifts?
- How does this passage relate to the whole subject of judgment?
- What is the potential risk of waiting until later in life to obey God?
- What specific changes do these parables motivate you to make in your daily routine?

RELIGIOUS LEADERS PLOT TO KILL JESUS

Matthew 26:1-5, Mark 14:1-2, Luke 22:1-2

Additional Information

At this time, Jesus was probably staying with Mary, Martha, and Lazarus. As Passover approached, the religious leaders assembled to figure out a way to kill Jesus, without turning the crowds against them. They met in the palace of Caiaphas who had served for eighteen years as the ruling high priest. He claimed that Jesus' death was necessary to "save" the nation of Israel from the wrath of Rome

(John 11:49-50). Although the Romans gave the Jews some freedom, they would also discipline their subjects if they didn't quietly obey and respect Rome's authority. The religious leaders were scared that the Romans would notice the disturbance Jesus' miracles were causing among the people and retaliate by punishing them or revoking some of their privileges.

Additional Questions

- What was going on behind the scenes in Jerusalem?
- Why were the religious leaders secretly plotting to do away with Jesus?
- How do you think they rationalized their plan to kill Jesus?

A WOMAN ANOINTS JESUS WITH PERFUME

Matthew 26:6-13, Mark 14:3-9, John 12:1-8

Additional Information

When Jesus and His disciples arrived in Bethany, they dined at the home of Simon the Leper (so called because Jesus had probably healed him of leprosy). It was an occasion when Simon wanted to honor Jesus.

The anointing of special guests and rabbis at wedding feasts was customary in Israel, but a costly gift such as Mary's was usually reserved for kings. Also, it was poured on their heads, not their feet. Mary broke the alabaster jar and emptied its contents both on Jesus' head (Matthew and Mark) and His feet (John). Without realizing it, she had prepared Jesus' body for death and burial.

Because the culture generally considered it immodest for a woman to wear her hair loose, some scholars believe that Mary of Bethany had been a loose woman before she met Jesus some years earlier. But this isolated incident should not brand Mary as such, nor identify her as Mary Magdalene.

Additional Questions

- What is the relationship of Mary's act of devotion to the preaching of the gospel (Matthew 26:13, Mark 14:9)?
- How do you think some people could misinterpret Jesus' statement about the poor in this passage?
- For what selfish reasons do people help the needy?
- How can we guard against improper motives?
- What sacrifices are sometimes necessary to help the poor?

JUDAS AGREES TO BETRAY JESUS

Matthew 26:14-16, Mark 14:10-11, Luke 22:3-6

Additional Information

"'What are you willing to give me if I hand Him over to you?' he [Judas] asked. Naturally the chief priests 'were glad' (Mark 14:11) when they heard these words. Here, just when they were in a quandary, thinking perhaps that the crowds of Jewish Passover pilgrims were rather solidly on the side of Jesus. The chief priests must have considered this an answer to their prayers. . . . Right there, on the spot, the deal was finalized, the money paid. . . .

"They knew very well that if Judas had the money 'in his pocket' he would not have dared to back out before committing the deed. . . .

"For the price of a slave, gored by an ox, the Savior was sold to His enemies. See Exodus 21:32. For such a pitiful sum Judas betrayed the Master!"[3]

Additional Questions

- Why did Judas's arrival change the plans of the religious leaders (see Matthew 26:3-5)?
- Do you think Judas had long contemplated this act, or was it a spur-of-the-moment decision?
- What characteristics or events brought Judas to the point where he could betray the Lord?

NEXT TIME: "Go for it!" "Look out for number one." "You deserve it." We are bombarded with messages from the world telling us to do whatever it takes to make us happy. But Jesus has given us very different instructions. In the next lesson, you will compare the priorities of God's Kingdom to the world's values. Jesus' example will also remind you of the importance of humble service.

LESSON FOUR
SERVICE WITH A SMILE

Jesus knew that one of His own disciples, Judas, would soon betray Him and turn Him over to be crucified. He also knew Peter, a disciple whom He deeply loved, would deny that he even knew Him. All of Jesus' closest friends would desert Him in His darkest hour. Yet, despite the hurt this must have caused Jesus, He opened His heart to the disciples and showed them the "full extent of His love" for them.

OBJECTIVE: As a result of this lesson, participants will see the sharp contrast between Christ's priorities and the world's values. Their study of one of Christ's most selfless acts will also reveal what it means to be a true servant.

Opening Questions

- What do you enjoy most about dining out?
- How do we usually determine how much money to leave for a tip at restaurants?
- In what other situations do we expect to be served?
- How do we typically react if we feel we haven't been served well?

DISCIPLES PREPARE FOR THE PASSOVER

Matthew 26:17-19, Mark 14:12-16, Luke 22:7-13

Additional Information

> "The usual proceedings at the Passover meal were an opening prayer for blessing, the recitation of the story of the Passover from Exodus 12, the singing of Psalms 113 and 114 (the 'Little

Hallel'), and the eating of the sacrificed lamb. The meal was concluded with a prayer of thanks and the chanting of Psalms 115-118 (the 'Great Hallel'). During the meal, the participants ate unleavened bread and bitter herbs and drank wine."[4]

Additional Questions

- How did Jesus tell the disciples to prepare for the Passover?
- How did the disciples respond to Jesus' instructions?
- How did Jesus once again indicate to His disciples that the end was near?
- What is the connection between the Passover and Jesus' death (see 1 Corinthians 5:7)?
- What command of Christ's do you need to obey this week?

JESUS WASHES HIS DISCIPLES' FEET

John 13:1-20

Additional Information

One scholar has written, "The disciples' minds were preoccupied with dreams of elevation to office in the coming kingdom. . . . Consequently, no one of them was likely to abase himself by volunteering to wash the feet of the others. They were ready to fight for a throne, but not for a towel."[5]

Additional Questions

- What was the significance of the dialogue between Peter and Jesus (John 13:6-10)?
- How did Peter respond to Jesus' actions?
- What character principle was Jesus teaching His disciples?
- What is a contemporary example of this?
- For what reasons do we often hesitate to serve others?
- Following Christ's example, what humble act of service could you do today?

JESUS FORETELLS HIS BETRAYAL AND SUFFERING

Matthew 26:20-25; Mark 14:17-21; Luke 22:14-16,21-30; John 13:21-30

Additional Information

In this culture, sharing a meal with someone meant more than simply satisfying one's hunger—it was a sign of trust between friends. Yet, Judas joined the disciples and Jesus at the last supper, all the while knowing that he would betray the Lord. Jesus revealed Judas as His betrayer by saying, "The one who has dipped his hand into the bowl with me will betray me." (While reclining at a table, it was customary to dip a piece of bread or meat into a bowl of sauce.) Jesus explained that the Son of Man would fulfill the prophecies that had been written about Him years earlier. He was probably referring to the passage in Isaiah 53 that describes the suffering of God's servant.

Additional Questions

- ▶Why do you think Jesus told the disciples at this time that one of them would betray Him?
- ▶Why did Jesus reveal to Judas that He knew he was planning to betray Him?
- ▶How could Judas, who knew the Lord so intimately, have betrayed Him?
- ▶Do you think Judas ever truly believed in Christ as the Messiah? Why, or why not?

NEXT TIME: Christ has invited you to come to His table. In the next lesson, you will gain a better understanding of what communion symbolizes and how to prepare for and participate in this important celebration.

LESSON FIVE
COME TO THE TABLE

"The Wednesday of that week seems to have been spent by Jesus in seclusion, either in Bethany or among the hills. At the hour of the Paschal feast, only a brief hour or two now, and the storm would break in devastating fury; but here in this quiet upper room the very peace of God was reigning. Here the great Christian Sacrament of all the ages was instituted."[6]

OBJECTIVE: As a result of this lesson, participants will discover the true meaning of communion as they study Jesus' words and actions at the last Passover meal He celebrated with the disciples.

Opening Questions

▸In what ways does sharing a meal unify a group of people?
▸How can remembering the past give people hope for the future?
▸How do you celebrate communion at your church?

JESUS AND HIS DISCIPLES HAVE THE LAST SUPPER

Matthew 26:26-28, Mark 14:22-24, Luke 22:17-20

Additional Information

After Judas had gone, Jesus brought a new element into the traditional celebration of the Passover meal by instituting a New Covenant remembrance of what He was about to do. Three of the Gospels record the Lord's Supper, as does 1 Corinthians 11:23-26. All of these accounts include the taking of the bread and cup, the prayer of blessing, and Jesus' explanation of how the blood relates to the covenant. Only the passages in Luke and 1 Corinthians record Jesus' instructions to believers to continue celebrating the Lord's Supper.

Additional Questions

- What is the meaning behind the elements used in the Lord's Supper?
- Why does Jesus want us to remember His death when we worship Him?
- What is the "new covenant" of which Christ's blood is the seal?
- What was the "old covenant" that it replaced?
- What does Paul add to the understanding of the Lord's Supper in 1 Corinthians 11:23-26?
- What does participating in Holy Communion mean to you?

JESUS TALKS WITH HIS DISCIPLES ABOUT THE FUTURE
Matthew 26:29-30, Mark 14:25-26, John 13:31–14:31

Additional Information

John describes the last few moments of the Lord's Supper in much greater detail than the other Gospel writers. According to his account, Jesus spent His final minutes encouraging the disciples to trust in God. He gave them a new commandment to love each other in the same way that He had loved them. Leviticus 19:18 commanded God's people to love their neighbors as themselves, but Jesus demonstrated a much greater love. On the cross, Jesus would show His love for all people, even those who crucified Him! Jesus also warned the disciples that the end was near. He knew that in the next few hours the disciples would feel totally defeated, so Jesus assured them that, despite all appearances, He would have victory over death.

After Jesus and the disciples finished the Passover meal, they sang a hymn, probably the second half of the Hallel Psalms (Psalm 115–118). Then they went to the Garden of Gethsemane on the Mount of Olives, directly east of Jerusalem. This was one of Jesus' favorite places (Luke 22:39, John 18:2).

Additional Questions

- What does it mean to love others as Christ has loved us (John 13:34-35)?
- Why is this love called a "new" commandment?

- ▸What implications does this new commandment have for your life today?
- ▸What is the relationship between obedience and love in the Christian life?
- ▸Why can't unbelievers receive the Holy Spirit?
- ▸What role does the Holy Spirit play in the lives of believers?
- ▸How do Jesus' words encourage us to stand firm in our faith?

JESUS PREDICTS PETER'S DENIAL

Matthew 26:31-35, Mark 14:27-31, Luke 22:31-38

Additional Information

On their way to the Garden of Gethsemane, Jesus told the disciples that they would soon desert Him. He singled out Peter, predicting that before the rooster crowed at dawn, Peter would deny Him three times. Peter vehemently protested, claiming he was ready and willing to die for Christ. In fact, all of the disciples pledged their loyalty to Jesus.

Jesus' calm demeanor and steady trust in God's will shine through at this moment. Luke records Christ's words to Simon Peter, "But I have prayed for you, Simon, that your faith may not fail." Jesus knew that Peter's denial would not destroy his faith, but would actually strengthen his commitment to Christ and prepare him to lead other believers.

Additional Questions

- ▸What does Peter's confidence that he would be willing to die with Christ and the disciples' confidence that they would not desert Him reveal about their understanding of the situation? (See also John 13:37-38, spoken earlier.)
- ▸What countered Satan's desire to destroy Peter (Luke 22:31-34)?
- ▸For what reasons do people today reject or deny Christ?
- ▸If we fall away and deny the Lord, what is the way back to fellowship?

JESUS TEACHES ABOUT THE VINE AND THE BRANCHES

John 15:1–16:4

Additional Information

Jesus had given His disciples a new commandment, and described to them His divine relationship to the Father. He then talked about the continuation of the intimate relationship He would have with His disciples using the metaphor of the vine and branches, a symbol of true Israel (see Jeremiah 2:21). Jesus presented Himself as the true messianic vine planted by God.

Additional Questions

- Why do you think Jesus chose this time to speak about the vine and the branches?
- What does it mean to "abide in Christ's love"?
- What kind of fruit is Jesus talking about in this passage?
- Why will the world hate Jesus' disciples (John 15:18-27)?
- What should be the Christian's response to the world's hatred?

NEXT TIME: It's easy to say that if we had been in the disciples' shoes on the night of Christ's arrest, we would have stood up for Him. But as you study the actions of Jesus' disciples in the next lesson, you will be challenged to think of ways your faith is tested. Christ's words of warning and encouragement to His disciples will show us how to remain loyal to Him.

The Cross and Resurrection

LESSON ONE

FICKLE OR FAITHFUL?

Jesus had already endured criticism, opposition, and mistreatment, but now the specific redemptive sufferings were about to begin in all their horror. The religious leaders and the Romans represented all men of all the ages as they heaped shame and suffering on Him. Truly He was about to become "the Lamb of God, who takes away the sin of the world" (John 1:29).

OBJECTIVE: As a result of this lesson, participants will recognize the ways their faith is tested and will learn how to stay loyal to Christ.

Opening Questions

- If you knew you only had one day left to live, with whom would you want to spend your last hours? Why?
- In what ways are your friendships tested?
- What words do you think your friends would use to describe you?

JESUS TEACHES ABOUT THE HOLY SPIRIT AND PRAYER

John 16:5-33

Additional Information

The disciples were relieved that Jesus was finally "speaking clearly and without figures of speech." They believed that He was from God and that He knew everything that was about to take place. They listened carefully as Jesus spoke about the future in this last discourse.

Jesus told the disciples what they could expect from a hostile world, and what would happen in it. He also assured them of the comfort and help of the Holy Spirit. In addition to comforting believers, Jesus explained that the Holy Spirit would convict the world of sin and prod people to repentance. The Spirit would also reveal God's priorities and values to believers. Though the disciples didn't completely understand Jesus' promises until later, when they were anointed at Pentecost, Jesus assured them that the Holy Spirit would tell them what to expect and what to do at the proper time.

Additional Questions

- What kind of persecution did Jesus predict for His disciples?
- What reasons did Jesus give for the persecution that was to come?
- In John 16:7-15, how did Jesus say the Holy Spirit would relate to the apostles, the world, and Himself?
- What did Jesus mean by His statement in John 16:16?
- How did Jesus explain to His disciples His coming death and the benefits it would bring them (John 16:17-33)?

JESUS PRAYS FOR HIMSELF AND BELIEVERS
John 17:1-26

Additional Information

> "The intercessory prayer of Jesus was offered at the close of His last discourse and charge to the apostles. . . . The place must have been somewhere between the upper room where they had celebrated the Passover, and the Garden of Gethsemane where He was later arrested. . . .
>
> "The prayer was not offered mentally or in private, but for the benefit of the apostles. It reflected much of the thought and needs referred to in the discourse that preceded it. It is therefore highly beneficial and challenges our most careful consideration. We tread on holy ground as we seek to understand and interpret it."[1]

Additional Questions

- In what ways was Jesus to be glorified?
- How did Jesus glorify His Father?
- From the statements Jesus made, what can we learn about God's purpose for the world?

- What can we learn about Christ's mission on earth?
- What does this prayer teach us about ourselves—our needs, our potential, our destiny?
- Of all the requests made by Jesus in this prayer, what seem to be the deepest concerns of His heart at this time?
- What can we learn about Christ's relationship with His Father in this prayer?

JESUS AGONIZES IN THE GARDEN

Matthew 26:36-46, Mark 14:32-42, Luke 22:39-46, John 18:1

Additional Information

Consider this insight: "It is not without a mystic significance that St. John alludes to the crossing of the Kidron [by Jesus and the disciples]. It was no pleasant stream. The sacrificial blood wherewith the Temple's altars were sprinkled, drained into it, and it was running red with the blood of the paschal lambs as the Lamb of God passed over it."[2]

Additional Questions

- What do you think was the agony of Gethsemane?
- Why did Jesus ask Peter, James, and John to go with Him into the garden?
- Why did Jesus tell the disciples to wait while He prayed alone?
- What advice did He offer?
- What can you do when you discover that your "spirit is willing but the flesh is weak"?

JESUS IS BETRAYED AND ARRESTED

Matthew 26:47-56, Mark 14:43-52, Luke 22:47-53, John 18:2-11

Additional Information

A number of motives have been attributed to Judas for his betrayal of Jesus: love of money, jealousy, fear, and a desire to force Jesus' hand.

> "We are left with what was almost certainly the real motive—the man's bitter, revengeful spirit. Disappointment of his worldly hopes bred spite, and spite deepened into hatred. . . . Jesus, he knew, saw right through him. And that intensified the man's anger and vindictiveness. He began to toy with the thought of treachery. Once that thought had

found a lodging in his mind, the rest of the tempter's task was easy. . . . Only the deed itself now remained. But what evil spirit suggested the signal be arranged with his accomplices that night? It was the crowning touch of horror, the last point of infamy beyond which human infamy could not go, when out in the garden Judas betrayed his Master, not with a shout or a blow or a stab, but with a kiss."[3]

Additional Questions

- From the events of the betrayal, what character traits do you see in Judas, Peter, and Jesus?
- How do you explain the behavior of each of these men at this point?
- Why was Jesus able to face this crowd so calmly?
- How can we attain a Christlike attitude of calmness and strength in the face of adversity?

NEXT TIME: God has given each of us a conscience to help us determine right from wrong, but sometimes a guilty conscience can go into "overdrive" and eventually destroy a person! The next lesson will look at how Jesus' disciples dealt with the guilt of denying and betraying the Lord. We will learn some important principles about how to deal with guilt in our own lives from their examples.

LESSON TWO
PRESUMED GUILTY

✣

At a distance Peter watches the drama unfold. "To understand what happened between Gethsemane and Calvary, we must try to grasp quite clearly the reason why Jesus was subjected to a double trial. We call it a trial; in reality it was an inquisition, and the death sentence, when it was carried out, was nothing more or less than judicial murder."[4]

OBJECTIVE: As a result of this lesson, participants will understand some principles they can follow when dealing with guilt in their own lives.

Opening Questions

▸When have you ever been unfairly accused? How did you feel?

▸In what different ways do people react to the injustice in the world?

JESUS IS QUESTIONED AND CONDEMNED

Matthew 26:57,59-68; 27:1; Mark 14:53,55-65; 15:1; Luke 22:54,63-71; John 18:12-14,19-24

Additional Information

"Jesus appeared first before the Jewish Sanhedrin: this was the civil trial. Had the charge on which Jesus appeared not been a capital one, the Sanhedrin alone could have decided the matter, without referring it to Pilate at all. For in Judea, as in all the provinces of her far-flung empire, Rome gave the conquered people a fair measure of self-government; and the judicious application of this Home Rule principle contributed largely to the maintenance of peace throughout her dominions. But where death sentences were involved, as in the case of Jesus, Rome reserved the final right of judgment to herself. Such cases, after going through the Jewish court, had to come up again for review before the Roman authorities, who had the power either to [approve] the verdict already pronounced and execute sentence on the accused, or to overturn the proceedings altogether and set the prisoner free. This explains what happened on the night of Christ's arrest."[5]

Additional Questions

- What do Jesus' responses during the Jewish trials reveal about His character?
- In what ways was this trial an unjust one?

PETER DENIES KNOWING JESUS

Matthew 26:58,69-75; Mark 14:54,66-72; Luke 22:54-62; John 18:15-18,25-27

Additional Information

"All the gospels give the sad account of the denials of Peter, but in varying order. The denials cover some time, more than an hour at least during the illegal and informal ecclesiastical trials before Annas and Caiaphas. . . . After the panic, in which all the eleven had left Jesus to His enemies in Gethsemane, two had gained courage enough to turn back and follow the arresting party as it was leading Jesus away to the palace of the high priest on the west side of the city. John, whose name is not revealed, came up with the band and entered in immediately on arrival, being a personal acquaintance of the high priest, probably through business relationships when he was in the fishing firm in Capernaum. Peter, in spite of his previous boast that he would follow Him even to death and his reckless assault on Malchus, servant of the high priest, in the hour of arrest, 'was following the party now afar off.' There were others of the twelve who did not follow at all, but went and hid themselves for fear of the officers. Peter was a leader and bore a greater responsibility. Though he was filled with dread and fear at this hour, he yet loved his Master."[6]

Additional Questions

▶If Peter could have somehow lived this experience over again, what do you think he would have done differently?

▶What do you think Peter learned from his failure?

▶What emotions do you think Peter felt at different times throughout this experience?

▶What precautions can we take to make sure we don't forsake our beliefs when times get tough?

JUDAS KILLS HIMSELF

Matthew 27:3-10, Acts 1:18-19

Additional Information

The religious leaders would not take back Judas's money. Jewish law prohibited money gained by unlawful means to be used in the temple. After Judas's death, the religious leaders bought a parcel of land in Judas's name (Acts 1:18-20). Such irony! The chief priests could pervert their own system of laws to condemn an innocent man (all the trials of Jesus were illegal), but they refused to accept Judas's money because it was against the law!

Additional Questions

▶Read Matthew 26:69-75 and 27:3-10 to compare the characters and responses of Peter and Judas. What differences and similarities do you see in these two disciples?

▶What double standard do you see demonstrated by the religious leaders?

JESUS STANDS TRIAL BEFORE PILATE AND HEROD

Matthew 27:2,11-31; Mark 15:1-20; Luke 23:1-25; John 18:28–19:16

Additional Information

> "When Caiaphas and his satellites had done their work, Jesus was marched off to the Roman governor for the second stage of His trial. Pontius Pilate had now been procurator for

six years, and had found the post by no means [an easy job]. The Crown Colony of Judea was one of the most difficult and turbulent corners of the Emperor Tiberius' vast dominions. But Pilate's unnecessarily harsh and relentless ways of dealing with the administrative problems that were continually confronting him had made him anything but popular with the people he had to govern. He despised the Jews, and failed altogether to appreciate the religious traditions of their race. They had not forgotten the day when, in open defiance of Jewish sentiment and in flagrant breach of the conciliatory policy which Rome officially sanctioned, Pilate had caused images of Caesar as god to be carried through the streets of the Holy City. Nor had they forgotten certain other occasions when he had read the Riot Act and sent his soldiers in amongst the crowds, and caused bloodshed and massacre (Luke 13:1). Neither the Sanhedrin nor the mass of common people had much love for Pilate; but the spur of necessity works wonders, and it was now the main hope of Caiaphas and the rest to make a good impression on their governor and win him to their side, and so secure the death of Jesus."[7]

Additional Questions

- What seemed to be the major charges against Jesus?
- In what sense is Jesus' Kingdom not of this world?
- Why did Pilate offer a choice between Barabbas and Jesus?
- What did Pilate really think about Jesus?
- What do you think caused the change in the crowds (see Mark 11:1-11, 15:6-15)?
- Why do you think Jesus refused to answer Herod?
- What do you think went through the minds of the disciples as they watched Jesus being ridiculed in the trials?

NEXT TIME: Jesus was all alone—the disciples deserted Him and the religious leaders condemned Him to death. The Son of God prepared Himself to endure the ultimate pain of the cross. As you study Christ's death and resurrection in the next lesson, you will learn the reason for and true meaning of these momentous events and the difference they can make in your life today.

LESSON THREE

THE FINAL STEP

"Here it may be well to remind ourselves of what death by crucifixion meant in the thoughts of the ancient world. With the passing of the years, Christendom has cast a halo of beauty round the cross. . . . But all this ought not to hide from us the fact that originally the cross was a thing unspeakably shameful and degrading. . . . Devised in the first instance in semi-barbaric Oriental lands, death by crucifixion was reserved by the Romans for slaves and for criminals of the most abandoned kind."[8]

OBJECTIVE: As a result of this lesson, participants will learn the reason for and true meaning of the crucifixion and resurrection and how these events affect our lives now.

Opening Questions

- How are criminals punished today?
- In your opinion, what is the most humiliating punishment for a terrible crime?
- What do you think it would be like to be on "death row"?

JESUS IS CRUCIFIED

Matthew 27:31-56, Mark 15:20-41, Luke 23:26-49, John 19:16-37

Additional Information

Crucifixion was the Roman method of execution, used only with slaves and foreigners, never with Roman citizens. Generally it took days for a man to die on a cross—days of excruciating pain.

> "Historically, the Roman custom of crucifying was crucifixion completely without clothing. The humiliation included being naked. It is amazing that in Psalm 22, before crucifixion had ever been used as a means of death, the description of it is so clear. . . . The Trinity had chosen and planned the manner and time of the death. . . . This is an exchange. Yes, He really hung there, making all these exchanges possible. And while He was suffering, He prayed for the men who put Him there."[9]

For a detailed, prophetic account of the crucifixion, read Psalm 22:14-18.

Additional Questions

- What are some implications we can draw from Jesus' seven statements on the cross (Luke 23:34,43; John 19:26-27; Matthew 27:46; John 19:28,30; Luke 23:46)?
- What do you think each of the signs accompanying the death of Jesus meant (Matthew 27:51-56)?
- In looking at the other people involved in this event, what common human behavior traits do you see?
- What importance do you see in the statement, "He saved others, but He can't save Himself" (Matthew 27:42)?
- What does Jesus' statement "It is finished" mean for us today?
- In what way did God forsake Jesus?
- In what sense are believers today called to bear Christ's cross?

JESUS IS BURIED

Matthew 27:57-66, Mark 15:42-47, Luke 23:50-56, John 19:38-42

Additional Information

Jesus died at approximately three o'clock in the afternoon, and His followers had until about six o'clock to bury His body before the official Sabbath would begin. It was unlawful to leave a body on a tree overnight (Deuteronomy 21:23) and could never be done on the Passover Sabbath. Pontius Pilate, assured by the centurion that Jesus was dead (Mark 15:44), granted Joseph's request for the body. With help, he took Jesus' body off the cross.

Joseph furnished linen wrappings and his new tomb (Matthew 27:60), and Nicodemus provided myrrh and aloes. (One hundred *litrai* would be equivalent to about seventy-five pounds or thirty-four kilograms.) As the two men wound the linen wrappings around the body, they poured in the mixture of spices in compliance with the Jewish manner of preparing their dead for burial. Jesus' burial in Joseph's tomb fulfilled yet another Old Testament prophecy (Isaiah 53:9).

Additional Questions

- How did Pilate confirm Jesus' death (Mark 15:44-45)?
- Why is this significant?
- Where was Jesus buried?
- Why did the Jewish religious leaders obtain a guard for Jesus' tomb (Matthew 27:62-66)?
- How does the Gospel writer describe Joseph (Luke 23:50-51)?
- What does Luke mention about the women at the burial site?
- Why do you think Luke included this detail in his account?

JESUS RISES FROM THE DEAD AND APPEARS TO THE WOMEN *Matthew 28:1-15, Mark 16:1-11, Luke 24:1-12, John 20:1-18*

Additional Information

> "[Jesus followers] had clung . . . to their Jewish ideal and expected confidently that He would manifest Himself to the world in regal splendor, claim the throne of His father David, and reign in Jerusalem over the emancipated and regenerate Israel. The Crucifixion had dispelled their dream. . . . It seemed that nothing remained for them but to . . . resume the occupations which they had abandoned in quest of a Kingdom. They had fled panic-stricken when their Master was arrested, and their first impulse was doubtless to get back to Galilee. . . . They repented of their cowardice and, [returned] to the neighborhood of Jerusalem."[10]

Additional Questions

- Taking the role of a news interviewer, what questions would you ask to expose the lies of the guards (Matthew 28:11-15)?
- What questions come to your mind as you examine the account of Christ's resurrection and His first appearance to others?
- Why did those who saw the risen Christ respond first by worshiping Him?
- What emotions do you imagine they felt as they first saw Jesus alive again?

▶How do you account for the initial unbelief of the disciples when the women told them about the resurrection?

▶Why is Christ's resurrection so important for us (see 1 Corinthians 15:14-19)?

NEXT TIME: Sunday morning revealed a startling fact—the tomb in which Jesus had been buried was empty! The next lesson reveals how Jesus convinced the disciples that He had indeed risen from the dead as He had promised. As you study their responses to Jesus, you will be challenged to decide what you believe about Him.

THE CROSS AND RESURRECTION

LESSON FOUR
WE MEET AGAIN

✣

People respond to the story of Christ's resurrection in different ways. Some assume it's a lie, a fable that has been passed down through the generations. Others may demand scientific proof to back up the Gospel accounts. But only the Holy Spirit can fully reveal the significance of this spectacular event. As you sort out the facts of this story, ask God's Spirit to help you and your group better understand how this event is relevant to your lives today.

OBJECTIVE: As a result of this lesson, participants will see how the disciples were slowly convinced that Jesus had been raised from the dead. The disciples' testimony will challenge them to decide what they believe about Jesus.

Opening Questions

▶How does it feel to be reunited with a long-lost friend or relative?

▶When have you had a hard time believing a friend's story?

▶How do we usually determine whether a person is telling the truth?

JESUS APPEARS TO TWO BELIEVERS TRAVELING ON THE ROAD *Mark 16:12-13, Luke 24:13-35*

Additional Information

After Jesus' death, two disciples were walking to Emmaus and discussing all of the recent events that had taken place in Jerusalem. Not only were they despondent over Jesus' death, but they were saddened by the report of some women that Jesus' tomb was now empty. Instead of believing that Jesus had risen from the dead, they chose to wallow in their grief and disappointment.

Then Jesus Himself joined them, but they were kept from recognizing Him by divine intervention. Jesus explained to them that everything had happened exactly as the Scriptures had prophesied. Not until after they had shared a meal did the two finally realize that they were in the presence of the risen Lord! When God opened their eyes and they understood the significance of what they had seen, the two rushed back to Jerusalem to share the good news with the other disciples.

Additional Questions

- How did the disciples respond to the different phases of their discussion with Jesus?
- How do you think these two disciples felt as they told Jesus about the crucifixion and rumored resurrection of Jesus Christ?
- What was their attitude as Christ explained to them the Old Testament Scriptures?
- Why were their eyes opened when Jesus broke the bread?
- What impresses you most about how Christ revealed Himself to these two disciples?

JESUS APPEARS TO THE DISCIPLES BEHIND LOCKED DOORS *Mark 16:14, Luke 24:36-43, John 20:19-23*

Additional Information

After His encounter with the two disciples on the road to Emmaus, Jesus appeared to the eleven disciples (minus Judas Iscariot who had committed suicide). The eleven had locked themselves in a room to hide from the Jews who had turned on them since Christ's trial and crucifixion. Instead of criticizing them for their cowardice and desertion, Jesus addressed the group with a Hebrew greeting, "Peace be with you." The disciples initial reaction was fear and surprise—they thought He was a ghost. Jesus assured them that He was real, even though His body was different (He was able to suddenly appear in a locked room). Jesus showed the disciples the nail marks in His hands and feet and the wound in His side. He also ate a piece of fish to prove that he had a physical body. Finally, the disciples believed that Jesus had indeed risen from the dead and they were overjoyed!

Additional Questions

▶For what reasons do you think Christ ate fish with the disciples?

▶What instructions did Jesus give to His disciples at this time (John 20:21-23)?

▶What significance do you see in these instructions?

▶What part is the Holy Spirit to play in our lives?

▶What did Jesus mean when He said He was sending the disciples "as the Father has sent" Him?

▶Why did Thomas respond to the disciples' testimonies as he did (John 20:24-25)?

JESUS APPEARS TO THE DISCIPLES INCLUDING THOMAS
John 20:24-31

Additional Information

At this point it becomes difficult to trace the appearances of Jesus in the Gospel accounts. For example, in Luke's Gospel there is a forty-day gap between verses 43 and 44 of chapter 24; verse 43 takes place on the day of resurrection, while verse 44 takes place on the day of ascension. Therefore it is necessary to switch back and forth among the Gospels in order to get an accurate picture of the last forty days Jesus spent on earth.

Additional Questions

▶How does Thomas's response in this section compare with his earlier response (John 20:24-25)?

▶What does this passage demonstrate about Thomas and Jesus?

JESUS APPEARS TO THE DISCIPLES WHILE FISHING
John 21:1-25

Additional Information

Several of Christ's disciples worked to get perspective on the recent events. "In Jerusalem they had been in a strange city where unnerving events had followed each other with dizzy rapidity. . . . Galilee, however, was the same. The familiar haunts, the sight of the fishing boats rocking gently on the lake, the smell of fish, and the pressing need of food and occupation brought them to a crisis."[11] Having returned to Galilee, they began the rugged, hard work of fishing once again.

Jesus appeared to them again while they were fishing. In this third appearance to the disciples, Jesus paid special attention to Peter. Though Peter had failed the Lord, Jesus gave him another chance to prove his love and devotion. Jesus knew that Peter was truly repentant and was ready to serve Him with his life.

Additional Questions

- What is the significance of Jesus appearing to the men at this time?
- What does the fact that Jesus prepared breakfast for these men suggest to you?
- What questions did Jesus ask Peter?
- How would you respond if today Christ asked you these same questions?
- What commands does Jesus give to Peter, and what do they mean?
- What do you know about how Peter carried out these commands?

NEXT TIME: You've come a long way in this study on the life of Christ, but don't stop here! The next lesson will reveal Jesus' final words to His disciples before He ascended to Heaven. You'll discover how He wants *you* to be involved in fulfilling the Great Commission.

LESSON FIVE
SPREAD THE WORD!

✣

The eleven apostles returned to Galilee, where Jesus had promised to meet them (Matthew 26:32), and where the women, instructed by the angel and Jesus, had directed them to go (Matthew 28:7,10). When Jesus appeared to His apostles for the fourth time, He gave them what has become known as the Great Commission.

OBJECTIVE: As a result of this lesson, participants will discover how they can be involved in fulfilling the Great Commission.

Opening Questions

- When have you had such great news that you couldn't keep it to yourself?
- If you could travel back in time to the period between Christ's resurrection and ascension, what would you want to ask Jesus?

JESUS GIVES THE GREAT COMMISSION
Matthew 28:16-20, Mark 16:15-18

Additional Information

On previous missions, Jesus specifically instructed the disciples to minister only to Jews (Matthew 10:5-6). Now He commissioned them to spread the good news to all peoples in all parts of the world.

Jesus told them to baptize new believers "in the name of the Father and of the Son and of the Holy Spirit." When a Christian is baptized, he declares to the world that he wants to submit to

Christ's authority. Baptism doesn't provide salvation from sin, but symbolizes acceptance of God's grace through faith in Jesus Christ.

Additional Questions

- How does what Jesus accomplished in His time on earth relate to what He asks us to do in the Great Commission?
- How can we become disciplemakers?
- What part does the Holy Spirit play in disciplemaking?
- Which parts of this commission do you think are most difficult to obey?
- Are there any circumstances which would excuse a believer from taking part in the Great Commission? Why, or why not?
- How does Jesus' promise in this passage encourage you?

JESUS APPEARS TO THE DISCIPLES IN JERUSALEM

Luke 24:44-49, Acts 1:3-8

Additional Information

During this period Jesus repeated some of the same instructions He had given before in His pre-Calvary ministry, probably using the same method of teaching He had with the two disciples on the road to Emmaus. Jesus' vision for the accomplishment of the prophecy that "all the ends of the earth will see the salvation of our God" (Isaiah 52:10) is revealed in the Great Commission, repeated again just before the ascension.

Additional Questions

- What was Jesus' last instruction to His disciples before He ascended (Acts 1:8)?
- How were the disciples finally able to understand how Jesus fulfilled all the prophecies in Scripture about the Messiah?
- How has the Holy Spirit "opened your mind" to the truth of God's word?
- Why did the carrying out of the Great Commission begin in Jerusalem?
- What implications might this fact have for you personally as you participate in the Great Commission?
- In all, how many distinct appearances of Jesus are recorded?

JESUS ASCENDS INTO HEAVEN

Mark 16:19-20, Luke 24:50-53, Acts 1:9-12

Additional Information

The ascension took place on the Mount of Olives, across the Kidron valley from Jerusalem and the temple complex. This hill was a Sabbath day's journey—about 2,000 cubits (just over half a mile or less than one kilometer)—from the capital city. After Jesus ascended to Heaven, two angels joined the disciples, promising that Jesus would return in the same manner. So the disciples returned to Jerusalem to wait for the coming of the Holy Spirit.

Additional Questions

- What principle or truth from this lesson do you feel God wants you to apply to your life? How?
- How does the full story of Christ's life serve as an example of what our lives should be like?
- How would you describe Jesus' personality and character to someone who had never read the Bible before?
- In what ways has this study of Christ's life and ministry changed your life?

NOTES

THE BEGINNING

1. Merrill C. Tenney, *New Testament Times* (Grand Rapids, Mich.: Eerdmans, 1965), p. 139.
2. Extrait de Henri Daniel-Rops, "La vie Quotidienne en Palestine au temps de Jesus," *Daily Life in the Time of Jesus*, Librairie Hachette Editeur, Paris, France. English edition published by Hawthorn Books (New York, 1962), p. 104.
3. Erich Sauer, *The Dawn of World Redemption* (Grand Rapids, Mich.: Eerdmans, 1951), p. 176.
4. George B. Eager, "Marriage," *The International Standard Bible Encyclopedia* (Grand Rapids, Mich.: Eerdmans, 1956), pp. 1997-1998.
5. David Smith, *The Days of His Flesh* (New York: Harper & Brothers, n.d.), p. 3.
6. David and Pat Alexander, ed., *Eerdmans' Handbook to the Bible* (Grand Rapids, Mich.: Eerdmans, 1973), pp. 138-139.
7. G. Campbell Morgan, *The Crises of the Christ* (Old Tappan, N.J.: Revell, 1903), pp. 98-99.
8. Bruce M. Metzger, *The New Testament, Its Background, Growth, and Content* (New York: Abingdon Press, 1965), p. 24.
9. J. W. Shepard, *The Christ of the Gospels* (Grand Rapids, Mich.: Eerdmans, 1939), pp. 40-41.
10. Tenney, *New Testament Times*, p. 144.

11. From *Jesus the Messiah* by Donald Guthrie, p. 3. Copyright © 1972 by The Zondervan Corporation. Used by permission.
12. From *Jesus the Messiah* by Donald Guthrie, p. 42. Copyright © 1972 by The Zondervan Corporation. Used by permission.
13. Shepard, *The Christ of the Gospels*, p. 90.
14. Edward B. Pollard, "Money-changers," *The International Standard Bible Encyclopedia* (Grand Rapids, Mich.: Eerdmans, 1956), pp. 2080-2081.
15. Shepard, *The Christ of the Gospels*, p. 93.

CHALLENGING TRADITION

1. R. V. G. Tasker, *The Gospel According to St. Matthew—An Introduction and Commentary* (Grand Rapids, Mich.: Eerdmans, 1961), p. 56.
2. J. W. Shepard, *The Christ of the Gospels* (Grand Rapids, Mich.: Eerdmans, 1939), p. 115.
3. Alfred Edersheim, *The Life and Times of Jesus the Messiah*, 2 volumes (Grand Rapids, Mich.: Eerdmans, 1962), vol. I, pp. 474-475.
4. From *The Training of the Twelve* by Alexander Balmain Bruce. Copyright 1928 by Doubleday, Doran & Company, Inc., pp. 11-12. Reprinted by permission of the publisher.
5. Edersheim, *The Life and Times of Jesus the Messiah*, vol. I, pp. 510, 513.
6. Shepard, *The Christ of the Gospels*, p. 176.
7. John R. Sampey, "Sabbath," *The International Standard Bible Encyclopedia* (Grand Rapids, Mich.: Eerdmans, 1956), p. 2631.
8. J. C. Lambert, "Beatitudes," *The International Standard Bible Encyclopedia*, p. 419.
9. Lambert, *The International Standard Bible Encyclopedia*, p. 419.
10. From *An Exposition of the Sermon on the Mount* by Arthur W. Pink, p. 49. Copyright 1950, 1953 by I. C. Herendeen. Reprinted by Baker Book House and used by permission.
11. From *Jesus the Messiah* by Donald Guthrie, p. 98. Copyright © 1972 by the Zondervan Corporation. Used by permission.
12. Merrill F. Unger, *Unger's Bible Handbook* (Chicago: Moody Press, 1966), p. 524.
13. Shepard, *The Christ of the Gospels*, p. 219.

THE MESSIAH

1. J. W. Shepard, *The Christ of the Gospels* (Grand Rapids, Mich.: Eerdmans, 1939), p. 234.

2. From *Jesus the Messiah* by Donald Guthrie, pp. 110-111. Copyright © 1972 by the Zondervan Corporation. Used by permission.
3. James Stalker, *Life of Christ* (Old Tappan, N.J.: Revell, 1909), p. 29.
4. William Bauer, "Corban" *The International Standard Bible Encyclopedia* (Grand Rapids, Mich.: Eerdmans, 1956), p. 709.
5. From *Jesus the Messiah* by Donald Guthrie, pp. 158-159. Copyright © 1972 by the Zondervan Corporation. Used by permission.
6. Shepard, *The Christ of the Gospels*, p. 289.
7. James S. Stewart, *The Life and Teaching of Jesus Christ* (Edinburgh: The Committee on Publications, the Church of Scotland, 1933), p. 116.
8. From *The Training of the Twelve* by Alexander Balmain Bruce, pp. 224-225. Copyright 1928 by Doubleday, Doran & Company, Inc. Reprinted by permission of the Publisher.

FOLLOWING JESUS

1. J. W. Shepard, *The Christ of the Gospels* (Grand Rapids, Mich.: Eerdmans, 1939), pp. 339-341.
2. Shepard, *The Christ of the Gospels*, p. 339.
3. Shepard, *The Christ of the Gospels*, p. 348.
4. J. McNicol, "The Gospel According to Luke," *The New Bible Commentary* (Grand Rapids, Mich.: Eerdmans, 1965), p. 851.
5. From *A Survey of the New Testament* by Robert H. Gundry, p. 164. Copyright © 1970 by Zondervan Publishing House. Used by permission.
6. Shepard, *The Christ of the Gospels*, p. 387.
7. Merrill C. Tenney, John: *The Gospel of Belief* (Grand Rapids, Mich.: Eerdmans, 1948), p. 166.

ANSWERING THE CALL

1. A. T. Robertson, *A Harmony of the Gospels* (New York: Harper & Brothers Publishers, 1950), p. 149, footnote.
2. From *Jesus the Messiah* by Donald Guthrie, pp. 260-261. Copyright © 1972 by the Zondervan Corporation. Used by permission.
3. J. W. Shepard, *The Christ of the Gospels* (Grand Rapids, Mich.: Eerdmans, 1939), p. 473.

FINAL TEACHINGS

1. J. W. Shepard, *The Christ of the Gospels* (Grand Rapids, Mich.: Eerdmans, 1939), p. 505.
2. Norval Geldenhuys, *Commentary on the Gospel of Luke* (Grand Rapids, Mich.: Eerdmans, 1951), pp. 527-528.
3. From *New Testament Commentary*: *The Gospel of Matthew* by William Hendriksen, pp. 902-903. Published 1973 by Baker Book House and used by permission.
4. Geldenhuys, *Commentary on the Gospel of Luke,* p. 560.
5. Merrill C. Tenney, *John: The Gospel of Belief* (Grand Rapids, Mich.: Eerdmans, 1948), pp. 198-199.
6. James S. Stewart, *The Life and Teaching of Jesus Christ* (Edinburgh: The Committee on Publications, the Church of Scotland, 1933), p. 163.

THE CROSS AND RESURRECTION

1. J. W. Shepard, *The Christ of the Gospels* (Grand Rapids, Mich.: Eerdmans, 1939), p. 562.
2. David Smith, *The Days of His Flesh* (New York: Harper & Brothers Publishers, n.d.), p. 455.
3. James S. Stewart, *The Life and Teaching of Jesus Christ* (Edinburgh: The Committee on Publications, the Church of Scotland, 1933), pp. 169-170.
4. Stewart, *The Life and Teaching of Jesus Christ*, p. 172.
5. Stewart, *The Life and Teaching of Jesus Christ*, pp. 171-172.
6. Shepard, *The Christ of the Gospels*, p. 578.
7. Stewart, *The Life and Teaching of Jesus Christ*, pp. 175-176.
8. Stewart, *The Life and Teaching of Jesus Christ*, p. 181.
9. Francis and Edith Schaeffer, *Everybody Can Know*, page 365. Copyright 1973 by Francis and Edith Schaeffer. American edition by Tyndale House Publishers, Wheaton, Illinois, 1974.
10. David Smith, *The Days of His Flesh* (New York: Harper & Brothers Publishers, n.d.), p. 508.
11. Merrill C. Tenney, *John: The Gospel of Belief* (Grand Rapids, Mich.: Eerdmans, 1948), p. 288.

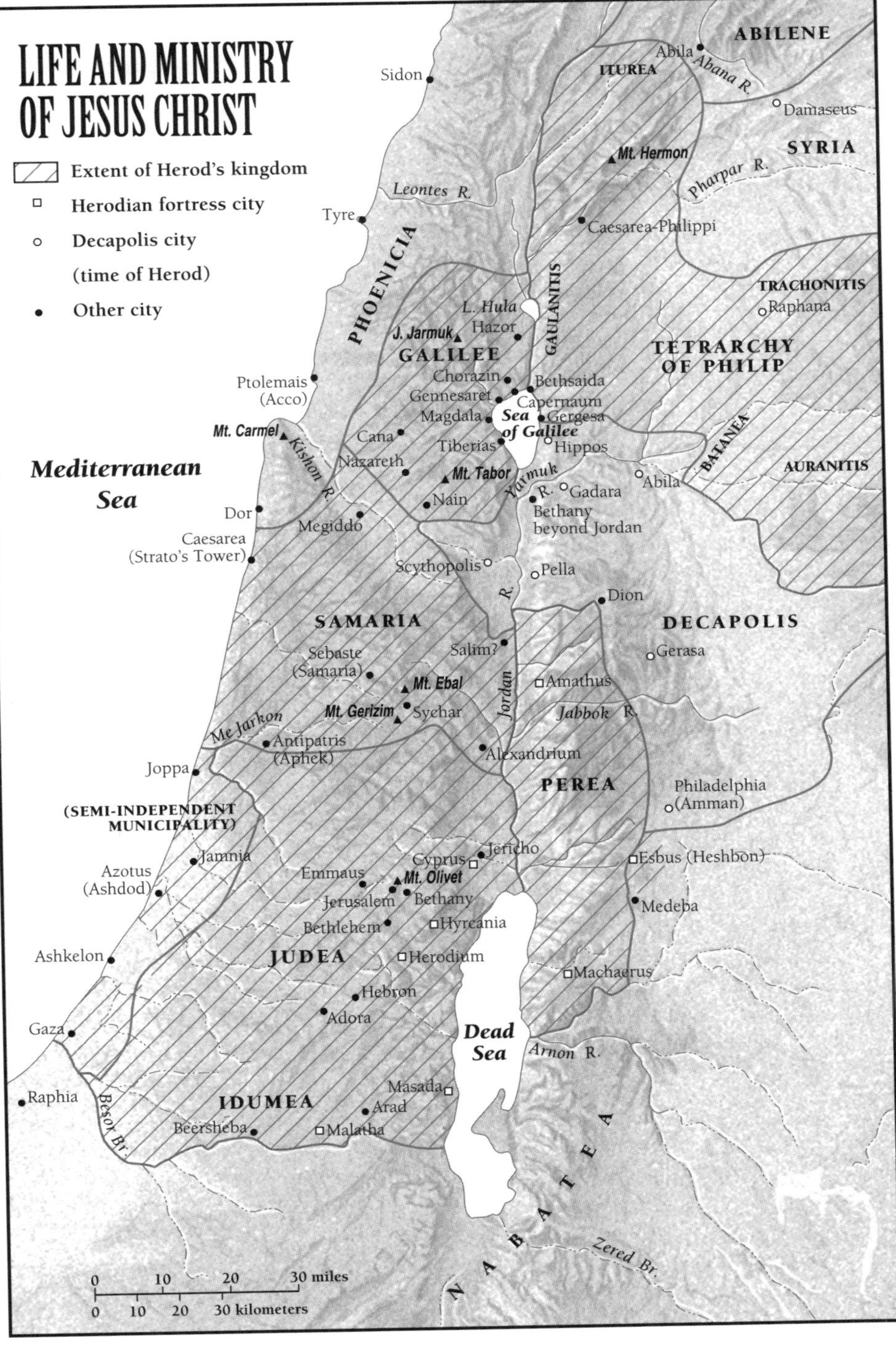
LIFE AND MINISTRY OF JESUS CHRIST
Extent of Herod's kingdom
Herodian fortress city
Decapolis city
(time of Herod)
Other city
ABILENE
Abila
Abana R.
ITUREA
Sidon
Damascus
Mt. Hermon
SYRIA
Pharpar R.
Leontes R.
Tyre
Caesarea-Philippi
PHOENICIA
GAULANITIS
TRACHONITIS
Raphana
L. Hula
Hazor
J. Jarmuk
GALILEE
TETRARCHY OF PHILIP
Chorazin
Bethsaida
Ptolemais
(Acco)
Gennesaret
Capernaum
Magdala
Sea of Galilee
Gergesa
Mt. Carmel
Cana
Tiberias
Hippos
BATANEA
Kishon R.
Mediterranean Sea
Nazareth
Mt. Tabor
AURANITIS
Yarmuk R.
Abila
Gadara
Nain
Dor
Megiddo
Bethany beyond Jordan
Caesarea
(Strato's Tower)
Scythopolis
Pella
Dion
Jordan R.
SAMARIA
DECAPOLIS
Salim?
Sebaste
(Samaria)
Gerasa
Mt. Ebal
Amathus
Mt. Gerizim
Sychar
Jabbok R.
Me Jarkon
Antipatris
(Aphek)
Alexandrium
Joppa
PEREA
Philadelphia
(Amman)
(SEMI-INDEPENDENT MUNICIPALITY)
Jericho
Cyprus
Esbus (Heshbon)
Jamnia
Azotus
(Ashdod)
Emmaus
Mt. Olivet
Jerusalem
Bethany
Medeba
Bethlehem
Hyrcania
Ashkelon
JUDEA
Herodium
Machaerus
Hebron
Adora
Gaza
Dead Sea
Arnon R.
Masada
Raphia
IDUMEA
Arad
Besor Br.
Beersheba
Malatha
NABATEA
Zered Br.
0 10 20 30 miles
0 10 20 30 kilometers

SMALL-GROUP MATERIALS FROM NAVPRESS

BIBLE STUDY SERIES

DESIGN FOR DISCIPLESHIP
GOD IN YOU
GOD'S DESIGN FOR THE FAMILY
INSTITUTE OF BIBLICAL COUNSELING Series
LEARNING TO LOVE Series
LIFECHANGE
RADICAL RELATIONSHIPS
SPIRITUAL DISCIPLINES
STUDIES IN CHRISTIAN LIVING
THINKING THROUGH DISCIPLESHIP

TOPICAL BIBLE STUDIES

Becoming a Woman of Excellence
Becoming a Woman of Freedom
Becoming a Woman of Prayer
Becoming a Woman of Purpose
The Blessing Study Guide
Homemaking
Intimacy with God
Loving Your Husband
Loving Your Wife
A Mother's Legacy
Praying From God's Heart
Surviving Life in the Fast Lane
To Run and Not Grow Tired
To Walk and Not Grow Weary
What God Does When Men Pray
When the Squeeze Is On

BIBLE STUDIES WITH COMPANION BOOKS

Bold Love
Daughters of Eve
The Discipline of Grace
The Feminine Journey
Inside Out
The Masculine Journey
The Practice of Godliness
The Pursuit of Holiness
Secret Longings of the Heart
Spiritual Disciplines
Tame Your Fears
Transforming Grace
Trusting God
What Makes a Man?
The Wounded Heart

RESOURCES

Brothers!
Discipleship Journal's 101 Best Small-Group Ideas
How to Build a Small-Groups Ministry
How to Lead Small Groups
Jesus Cares for Women
The Navigator Bible Studies Handbook
The Small Group Leaders Training Course
Topical Memory System (KJV/NIV and NASB/NKJV)
Topical Memory System: Life Issues